WOMEN AND FLIGHT

WOMEN AND FLIGHT

PORTRAITS OF CONTEMPORARY WOMEN PILOTS

CAROLYN RUSSO

Introduction by Dorothy Cochrane

The National Air and Space Museum
Smithsonian Institution
in association with
BULFINCH PRESS
LITTLE, BROWN and COMPANY
Boston • New York • Toronto • London

First edition

Library of Congress Cataloging-in-Publication Data
Russo, Carolyn.
    Women and flight : portraits of contemporary women pilots / photographs and text by Carolyn Russo ; introduction by Dorothy Cochrane. — 1st ed.
        p.   cm.
        ISBN 0-8212-2168-X. — ISBN 0-8212-2368-2 (pbk.)
    1. Women in aeronautics—United States—Biography. 2. Women air pilots—United States—Biography. 3. Women air pilots—United States—Portraits. 4. Women astronauts—United States—Biography. 5. Women astronauts—United States—Portraits. I. Cochrane, Dorothy. II. Title.
TL539.R87   1997
629.1'092'273—dc20
[B]   96-9541

Published by The National Air and Space Museum, Smithsonian Institution, in association with Bulfinch Press

Bulfinch Press is an imprint and trademark of Little, Brown and Company (Inc.)
Published simultaneously in Canada by Little, Brown & Company (Canada) Limited
Printed in the United States of America

Photographs for the book printed by Carolyn Russo
Book design by Charles O. Hyman and Anne Masters

Printed by Hull Printing
Bound by Acme Bookbinding

The Women and Flight traveling exhibition has been generously supported by Pratt & Whitney and United Technologies Corporation.

In-kind donations from Ilford Photo.

Funding for interview transcription by the Smithsonian Institution Women's Committee.

Traveling Exhibition by the Smithsonian Institution Traveling Exhibition Service

For
Joan Marie and Eva Louise

Contents

When Doris Lockness, an eighty-six-year-old active pilot with thirty-two great-grandchildren, directed me to the ultra-light aircraft and told me I was going for a ride I said, "No way, that's crazy." I didn't have her insatiable quest for thrill. A few moments later, I found myself in a "go-cart"-like aircraft, flying above the treetops before descending into a farmer's sprinkler, which splashed water across my face.

Her face lit only by the glow of a kerosene lamp, bush pilot Gayle Ranney told me airplane survival stories one night in her remote cabin in Yakutat, Alaska, as wolves and bears roamed outside. In my journey with this book, I stepped into the adventurous lives of thirty-six passionate American women pilots.

As a photographer working at the National Air and Space Museum, I pass by Amelia Earhart's Lockheed Vega, a symbol of the world's pioneer woman pilot, almost every day. So when a friend suggested I photograph women aviators, it seemed only natural. My initial research revealed little documentation on contemporary women pilots, giving me the incentive to compile this documentation for the National Air and Space Museum.

In 1992, I began searching for potential pilot candidates in magazines and newspapers. I also contacted aviation organizations and the military. Often, I relied on word-of-mouth recommendations from other pilots, as well as the invaluable suggestions from the staff at the National Air and Space Museum. Sometimes I found pilots by chance—after a three-year search for a crop duster, I drove by a crop dusting company whose owner told me about Lori Love. She just happened to be working in the same town.

Rather than focusing on the first, fastest, and most famous women, my goal was to document a vast range of pilots and to allow each pilot to tell her own story. The text in the pages following remains in the "spoken word" idiom to preserve each woman's unique voice as far as possible. The women I encountered while working on this project were not only generous with their time and aircraft, but their wisdom, and sometimes, friendship. Always, I walked away with more than a photograph. Astronaut Marsha Ivins took me to a place few people are allowed to visit—the top of the launch utility tower at the NASA Kennedy Space Center.

Driving away from a photography session with "Brothers to the Rescue" search and rescue pilot Mayte Greco, news came over the radio that her fellow pilots and friends had been shot down by the Cuban military. Despite her grief, she allowed me to accompany her to the organization's aircraft hangar later that night.

Although the women I interviewed followed different paths into the world of flight, I learned their common traits—they are brave, determined, and motivated. I believe the pilots portrayed in *Women and Flight* offer inspiration not only to the current and future generation of women pilots, but to all of us.

Carolyn Russo
Photographer, Smithsonian Institution
National Air and Space Museum

Introduction

BY DOROTHY COCHRANE

Freedom, challenge, the view from above, the excitement, the rush: these are among the reasons that people fly. The classic approaches to a life in aviation apply to the women profiled in these pages. Some who made that fateful decision worked many jobs to earn a license and win their chance to fly; they faced worlds of opportunity, danger, commitment, and determination; some were airport kids, pilots who remember the defining moment when the decision was made; and others just decided to try something new.

This group of aviators is extraordinary. Women are still newcomers to many sectors of aviation. *Women and Flight* explores the full spectrum of female aviators, from early barnstormers to aerobatic pilots, from cross-country pilots to space shuttle pilots. Who are they? Women who seemingly had no career paths in aviation, who encountered little encouragement and many barriers; women who created and are creating rich

Harriet Quimby, the first licensed American woman to fly, is posed for a formal portrait in the Marceau studio, New York, circa 1910–1912.

and rewarding life experiences; women who chose between flying and family; women who have reached outer space. Someday women pilots will be ordinary. But for now, until all the "firsts" are flown, they are still extraordinary.

Man first flew on December 17, 1903—man as a species and as a gender. Flying remained exclusively a male domain until Therese Peltier of France became the first woman to pilot an aircraft, in 1908. During the formative years of flight, women aviators were rare, and although they are a more common sight in the cockpit today, they remain a clear minority in aviation. How much progress has been made?

Women were not expected to participate in the world of oil-spattered pilots and wind-battered machines. Commanding a cockpit was considered a masculine role and thus inappropriate for a woman. In fact, the public's general perception was that women did not possess the intellect or temperament for flying. On the other hand, flight was such an exciting and extraordinary adventure that some people were equally thrilled to see women and men perform in the air.

Blanche Scott was one of a few determined women to receive formal flight training (offered by the Moisant, the Wright, or the Curtiss flying schools). Glenn Curtiss fitted the throttle of his Curtiss Pusher aircraft with a block to prevent Scott, his first woman student, from becoming airborne. Scott managed a short hop in the aircraft anyway and gained unofficial recognition as the first American woman to fly.

An early and very popular aviatrix was Harriet Quimby, who was the first American woman to receive a pilot's license. As part of the Moisant International Aviators, a popular flight exhibition team, Quimby won the admiration of the press and the public with her flying skills and her stylish beauty. The media raved over her plum-colored flying togs and assured itself, and everyone else, that she still indeed possessed feminine qualities. The gender issue was raised, however, when Quimby's own aviation adviser offered to disguise himself as Quimby and fly the English Channel for her. Quimby refused and made the flight herself in the spring of 1912, becoming the first woman to do so.

Pilots, male or female, had to be brave to fly those early machines. However, there were definite limits for women in the air. Women were not allowed to fly for the military, as the Stinson sisters, Katherine and Marjorie, and Ruth Law found out. Despite their successful exhibition careers and flying schools, military aviation was a barrier that could not be broken. In the end, only a handful of women piloted aircraft before World War I, and it appears that nearly all of them discontinued flying by the 1920s.

For some women, the barriers were doubled. Bessie Coleman was a young African American woman challenged by the notion of learning to fly. But discrimination in two forms, gender and race, forced her to seek training in France. There, in 1921, she became the first African American to receive a pilot's license.

The era between World War I and World War II is known as the golden age of flight. It was a time when pilots flew ever faster and sleeker aircraft around the pylons and explored uncharted territories of the earth. The world began to think of the airplane in practical, utilitarian terms, giving rise to aircraft companies and airlines. Although men dominated the emerging industry, women were significant participants. They flew in races, made extraordinary flights across thousands of miles of land and sea, set speed and altitude records, and sold aircraft. Phoebe Omlie, who had started her career as a barnstormer, worked for Monocoupe Aircraft Company demonstrating aircraft. Louise Thaden began as a salesperson for Beech Aircraft and then moved into racing (she became the first woman to win the prestigious Bendix Trophy, in 1936). Women demonstrating aircraft knew they were being used to push the old adage "If a woman can fly it, anyone can." However, they didn't mind, because they were flying airplanes and being paid for it. The Women's Air Derby of 1929 brought the best female pilots together for the first time. They proved to the public (and male aviators) their ability to fly cross-country.

Most female racers and record setters of the 1920s and 1930s — women such as Phoebe Omlie, Marvel Crosson, Mary Hazlip, Gladys O'Donnell, and Blanche Noyes—had supportive husbands who were also pilots. Others, like Pancho Barnes, chose aviation over marriage. Amelia Earhart wed her publicist, George Putnam, and together they promoted aviation. Few women had the resources to afford an airplane, so they relied on industry, endorsements, and family. Opportunities for women in aviation had to be carved out, for no real "career" niches existed.

Amelia Earhart's solo transatlantic flight of 1932 startled the world and still stands today as a testament to exceptional courage. Her unsuccessful world flight attempt five years later reflected her continuing need to stay current in the public eye in order to support herself in aviation. Jackie Cochran began flying as a businesswoman but quickly turned to racing and record setting. Earhart and Cochran both built their reputations through hard work and challenging flights.

While Earhart and Cochran stood foremost in the minds of Americans, other women were beginning to infiltrate the business and bureaucracy of flight, ensuring that women would indeed someday become an integral part of the aviation world. Blanche Noyes and Louise Thaden, among others, joined the National Air Marking Program, which was founded by Phoebe Omlie in 1934. This program of marking barns and buildings with names of towns and cities as navigation aids was the first federal program directed by a woman, with an all-woman top staff. Ruth Nichols began an air ambulance rescue business, Relief Wings, which was incorporated into the Civil Air Patrol during World War II. Olive Ann Beech cofounded Beech Aircraft with her husband, Walter, and worked side by side with him during the 1930s and 1940s. After his death, she became president and CEO, transforming the already successful company into its current status as a multimillion-dollar international aerospace corporation.

Still the barriers remained. In 1934, Helen Richey sought a career as a pilot with Central Airlines. She made seven flights in her first month, but only four over the next six months. The airline pilots' union refused her admission (without which she could only fly in good weather) and continually protested her presence in the cockpit. When

In 1921, Bessie Coleman became the first African American licensed pilot in the United States. After her flight training in France, she returned to America to pursue a career as a barnstormer. Coleman stands on the left wheel of a Curtiss JN-4. Date and location unknown.

it became clear that the job was a publicity sham, she resigned. Once the inevitability of World War II was recognized, the Civilian Pilot Training Program (CPTP) excluded women from training because CPTP pilots were expected to be drafted into the military. The few female instructors were, however, allowed to continue their work.

During World War II, women were utilized in a variety of support roles and industries, but as pilots, they were still questioned and even scorned. The creation of the Women Airforce Service Pilots (WASPs) was a struggle, until the absolute need for more pilots to ferry aircraft in the United States became obvious. The WASPs dramatically proved women's ability to fly every type of military aircraft, including the highly sophisticated P-51 Mustang and the legendary B-29 bomber. In all, 1,074 women flew more than 60 million miles in the service of their country; thirty-eight were killed. However, enthusiasm for the women pilots was not always shared by male pilots. Some felt that the women were getting publicity for routine ferrying missions that men flew unnoticed. When the WASPs were disbanded in 1944, with no military benefits, a few women found jobs in general and business aviation, but the great majority of them pursued completely different careers. Women's contributions to the postwar aviation effort were very limited: jobs were needed for men and women were needed at home.

The 1950s' mentality of the perfect housewife did little to stimulate an increase of women in aviation and major gender barriers still existed. Indeed, most women apparently preferred not to fly. But if they wanted to, and if they were qualified, what avenues were open to them? General aviation had no inherent barriers against women — it was a personal choice. The Ninety-Nines women pilots organization, founded in 1929, endured, and it sponsored the All-Women Transcontinental Air Races (dubbed "Powder Puff Derby" by the press). Betty Skelton was one of a handful of women who performed aerobatic maneuvers in airshows and competitions in the late 1940s and early 1950s. Women were found sporadically in general aviation, acting as instructors or fixed-base operators. Unfortunately, the general aviation boom expected after the war was a bust, and although Piper and Cessna were successful in reestablishing flying as a hobby for men in the 1950s, no one thought of encouraging women to fly. Economic and social factors continued to keep women from even considering jumping into a cockpit.

Some women pilots found entry-level positions in private industry, but they were few and far between. As in the 1930s, alliance with industry did provide opportunity. Jean Ross Howard-Phelan acquired her helicopter rating with the sponsorship of Bell Aircraft. However, as late as 1965, an editor of *Flying* magazine declared, "Aviation is, by and large, a masculine activity, and the woman who enters this arena does so at the risk of becoming less feminine."

There were no other options beyond private aviation. In the 1930s, commercial airlines first hired registered nurses to act as air hostesses, serving meals and caring for ill

....

Amelia Earhart poses in her flying gear, on the side of the Lockheed 5B Vega she used for her nonstop transatlantic flight on May 20–21, 1932.

13

passengers. It was hoped that by their very presence the nurses would calm passengers as well. However, as passenger service became routine and competition between airlines heated up, stewardesses became advertising bait, dressed in fashionable uniforms. Young women were seen as decorations for transport aircraft; hardly anyone was ready for a woman in the cockpit.

The military also had numerous restrictions against female participation in aviation, especially in the cockpit. In 1960, when a group of women pilots with several thousand hours of flying time passed preliminary physical and psychological tests similar to those required for the first Mercury astronauts, there was no real opportunity at hand. After all, astronauts were required to be test pilots, and only the military and their private contractors employed test pilots.

Ultimately though, times did change, thanks to the women's and civil rights movements. Armed with more education and greater economic independence, women began to fly in larger numbers, building up hours, becoming flight instructors, and acquiring ratings. Between 1960 and 1970, the number of licensed female pilots grew from 3.6 percent of all licensed pilots to 4.3 percent. Several women, including Jerrie Mock and Ann Pellegreno, made successful round-the-world flights.

With the aid of landmark changes in policy and law, the final barriers in commercial and military aviation, as in business and industry throughout the United States, have been broken over the last twenty-five years. The first fully vested U.S. female com-mercial airline pilot, Emily Warner, literally spent years at Continental Airlines' door, watching as her own male flight students were hired by airlines, until she was finally hired in 1973. Slowly women are building up their hours and making the move into the cockpit, and from right seat to left seat. Frequent flyers may encounter female pilots, though the sporadic tourist may not yet have seen her first female airline pilot. The public continues to be surprised, and even nervous, upon hearing a feminine voice say, "Good afternoon, ladies and gentlemen, this is your captain speaking."

The full integration of women into the cockpit in the military will also require a significant period of time. The U.S. Navy selected its first six noncombat female pilots in 1974, and the U.S. Army trained its first female pilot, Lieutenant Sally Murphy, the same year. The Air Force followed suit with training classes in 1976. Again, the accumulation of hours in all types of aircraft is the key to women's advancement. In 1991, the ban on women's flying combat aircraft was lifted, but in 1993, the U.S. Secretary of Defense was forced to order the military services to implement the decision. Old ways die hard, and invisible barriers must still be broken. Female military aviators understand the scrutiny they must bear, and they know they must perform impeccably to become fully accepted members of the flight team.

Fortunately, space has proven to be a more egalitarian environment. Although the media hype and genuine admiration of the Mercury seven astronauts generated wild enthusiasm, the all-male corps was not appreciated by everyone. The program initially perpetuated the military bias against women. However, following the conclusion of the Apollo program, the integration of women and other minorities into the space program began. The space shuttle program departs dramatically from the early manned-space programs, which sought to prove human and technological viability in space and focused on the race to the moon. The space shuttle is a working scientific laboratory for astronauts. Although many current astronauts are pilots, it is not a requirement, thus opening the field to a broad spectrum of qualified scientists. The astronaut class of 1978 included six women to be trained as mission specialists. In 1983, Sally Ride became the first American female astronaut to fly in space, and since then women have served on crews on a regular basis.

The intense team effort and total commitment to the shuttle program has allowed women to be absorbed into each individual flight and the entire program with minimal difficulty. Milestones continue to accumulate: Kathleen Sullivan became the first American woman to walk in space, in 1984; Judith Resnick and Christa McAuliffe became the first women to die in the space program, in 1986; Eileen Collins made the move to the pilot's seat of the shuttle in 1995. Perhaps movies and television programs on future space travel have prepared us, by showing us worlds not constrained by discrimination. In reality, though, the exploration of space began just as the playing field was being leveled and as young women were beginning to receive the proper education and encouragement.

According to the Federal Aviation Administration, the number of certificated female pilots in 1995 was 38,032, or just 6 percent of the total active certificated pilots in the United States. Though the figure is still disappointingly low, there is an encouraging note: 12.5 percent of student pilot certificates were held by women. The general aviation community has finally realized that it was missing, or ignoring, half the U.S. population. Therefore, concerted efforts to promote private flying are now aimed at the total population, young and old, men and women.

The women in this book entered aviation for a wide variety of reasons, at different times, and through different paths. They offer vivid demonstrations of personal courage and historical progress, and show what women can accomplish when given the same options as men. Women are now involved in every aspect of aviation, and the old biases and questions no longer apply, although they may still linger. Women pilots fly for fun, as always, but they may now enter any one of the major aviation theaters —commercial, corporate, military, and aerospace. Finally, women have a real choice and a real future in aviation. Opportunity is knocking.

Dorothy Cochrane
Curator, Aeronautics Department
National Air and Space Museum

ELLEN PANEOK

Alaskan Bush Pilot *Born October 17, 1959*

The elders call me Owl Eyes because I can see and fly in any type of weather. The Eskimos, they'll hop into the airplane with me without any hesitation. They trust me implicitly. Weather is the biggest danger of all in Alaska. It can change so fast, you can be out on a perfect day, going through a mountain pass, come around the corner, and the whole pass is just socked in, clogged up with a big cloud. If you don't have any room to turn around, you're dead.

In the wintertime we call it twenty-twenty weather—twenty below zero and twenty-knot winds. Our cutoff temperature for flying is thirty-five below zero, and you're talking *real* cold. I hate flying when it's that cold because your instruments fog up and your pen freezes. You have to sit there and do paperwork, so you have to warm up your pen. You have to do preflight in stages. You brush the snow and ice off the wings, the tail, and the prop, then go inside and have a cup of coffee and warm up. Then you go outside and put the seats in, go back inside and have another cup of coffee, and so forth.

You have to learn how to manage the engine to the point where you're not going to thermal shock the engine. Let's say if you're coming in to land, you don't just yank the throttle off to descend and land somewhere. You have to plan way ahead of time and bring the throttle back just a little bit at a time. On the manifold pressure, I'll bring it back two inches per mile. You won't have to worry about cylinders cracking in the cold or anything like that.

Let's say there's blowing snow at Point Leahy, and you can't see anything. Sometimes, when you're landing the only way you can find the runway is because it has strobes on the end of it, and in the wintertime they paint the middle of the runway hot pink, so you can see it in the blowing snow. I've landed there when I've been at one runway light and could just barely see the next one, and that's pretty crappy.

....

Ellen Paneok sitting on her polar bear "Harry" and displaying ivory and tools used for carving. Wasilla, Alaska, 1993.

Ellen Paneok is a Native American Eskimo pilot. She started flying in 1976 and has worked primarily in Point Barrow, Alaska, where she was chief pilot for Barrow Air, Inc., and also flew for Mark Air, and Cape Smythe, delivering supplies and U.S. mail to remote Eskimo villages in extreme weather conditions. Her talent in native ivory carving provides her additional income to purchase airplanes and parts. Once considered a rebel by the Federal Aviation Administration, she now lectures on safety issues for various aviation organizations. She was interviewed in Wasilla, Alaska, where she was living on a community airstrip and restoring antique airplanes.

After a big snowstorm when the weather is really bad and the runway gets clogged up with snowdrifts, all the village stores run out of milk, and the shelves get bare real fast, because the stores aren't that big anyway. They are really glad to see me. Up there, we used to call them P&P flights, and that's pop and Pampers. I shipped out so much pop and Pampers, it wasn't even funny. I could take in a thousand pounds of mail in a load, and then have the airplane seats tied up with me in the back, unload the mail, get seats set up, and put in six passengers in about seven minutes. When it's cold, you learn how to work fast.

I was born in the town of Kotzebue, thirty miles north of the Arctic Circle. It was mostly a subsistence type of lifestyle, with a lot of fishing and beluga whale and seal hunting. I grew up with fourteen people in a house the size of twenty by twenty feet. We didn't have running water then, so we had to go out to freshwater lakes to get ice. We bought clean trash barrels from the store, and we put ice in there and let it melt inside the house, and that's what we had for water.

My childhood after leaving Kotzebue was not good. We lived in the slums. My mom got divorced and didn't know how to live in the city by herself. She took to just leaving and left us alone quite a bit. A lot of times I didn't know where food was going to come from, and I was also taking care of my two younger sisters. One was a toddler and I was probably twelve years old. Being kids, we ended up eating a lot of macaroni with ketchup, and powdered eggs. And cheese. I think that was where I decided I wasn't

Ellen Paneok holding a vertical stabilizer to her Stinson SR-JR. Merrill Field Airport, Anchorage, Alaska, 1993.

going to like cheese, because that's what they gave us on welfare. Now I don't eat it, it just about makes me sick to my stomach.

I did not care at all whatsoever if I made it out of high school. I skipped school quite a bit and just didn't want to be there because the kids hassled me so much. Not just because I was an Eskimo but because I was "different," quiet, introverted, and being on welfare I wore hand-me-down clothes, and you stand out in a crowd. They ostracized me.

When I was fifteen, I picked up a flying magazine and thumbed through it. I don't know where, I just remember I picked it up and started looking at it and thought, "Well, I'm going to try this." I got to the point where I was going to do nothing else but fly. I picked up every magazine or article I could find on flying and just ate it up like a sponge. My family thought I was obsessed. They said I was totally nuts and screwed up to want to fly.

A couple of years later, for some reason a big lump sum of money came to us, like fifteen hundred dollars, from the Native Association. So I took my check, cashed it, and plunked the money down in a flight school and said, "Here, I want to learn how to fly."

Bush flying to me is flying a Beaver on floats on remote lakes, taking hunters and fisherman out, and hauling U.S. mail to remote villages where they would not get it any other way. The most challenging part is the off-airport work, like landing on the sandbars, landing on top of a mountain with big tires, maybe on a twenty-degree grade, landing uphill and taking off downhill—to me, that's the epitome of bush flying.

One time these people wanted me to come and pick them up with their caribou meat at this one fish camp, and this was on snow. They said, "There's a place where it's flat—and you can land, and it's nine hundred feet long." And I get there, and it's about four hundred feet long. Then those guys sat there and parked their stuff and all the caribou meat right at the end of this little four-hundred-foot strip. So I buzzed the heck out of them until they finally got the idea and they moved all their crap, and then I landed. It was so narrow that I couldn't turn around because I was on skis, so I just taxied out into the tundra, and I'm bumping around, turning back around, and they thought I was nuts. Then I got out of the airplane—it was a Cessna 185—and they all just stared at me. "Woman pilot?" I finally said, "Come on, let's go. The airplane's getting cold." But you never know what kind of strip you're going to run up against when you're doing that kind of bush flying. There's a couple of times I've gone places and I just absolutely refused to land there. They'd be peeved, but too bad. I'm not going to risk it and wreck myself or the airplane.

In the wintertime I wore my Eskimo mukluks, and those consisted of caribou skin with the fur facing outside up to the knee, and the bottoms are made of dried seal hide. And then I wore rabbitskin socks with wool socks and never had any problems up to thirty or forty degrees below zero. And then just a regular work parka with maybe a vest underneath and a big fur hat that went over my ears. Then I had regular gloves on the inside and I had big mittens made out of

....

Ellen Paneok holding the horizontal stabilizer of a Stinson SR-JR that she is restoring. Wasilla, Alaska, 1993.

21

beaver fur that go up to my elbow on the outside. And then you can't tell if I am a male or a female, so I wore perfume—$225 per ounce—and believe you me, they knew. I just felt like I wanted to save some of my own femininity, and that's the way I compensated for it.

One time I was out walking by myself, like a stupid idiot, on the ice, with a rifle. I had a seven-millimeter. I just kept walking because it was so nice. Then I felt the hair on the back of my neck raise up. I turned around, and about forty yards away here's this polar bear with his head down low, running at me, charging. What scared me the most was the fact that his eyes were staring right into mine and you can just see the intent to kill. I didn't even have time to raise the rifle. I just whipped it off my shoulder and kind of got it from the waist, and I shot the bear. I didn't even aim and got it just right almost between the eyes, and I know it was just pure luck. I sat there and said, "Whooah!" I sat down on the ice and just looked at this bear and thought, "Wow, it could have ate *me*." It was a good-tasting bear.

I was flying this Cherokee 6, and I picked up this passenger. I was taking him from Kiana to Kotzebue, and about halfway—I could smell alcohol on him, but he didn't appear to be drunk, so that's why I took him. But about halfway, he started getting obnoxious. Apparently, his drunkenness woke up. He undid his seat belt, yelled at me and screamed really obnoxious and lewd things, I kept telling him to sit down and shut up and put his seat belt on and he wouldn't. Then he started to grab for the

Ellen Paneok wearing an Eskimo parka made of white wolf fur. Wasilla, Alaska, 1993.

wheel, and that made me mad. I took the wheel and shoved it forward as much as I could. I rolled the airplane and did them sloppy on purpose so that he was flopping around inside the cockpit. I did a loop, and I fell out of the top of the loop and he fell. I stopped doing the aerobatics, and I just looked at him real calm. His eyes were all bugged out. I said, "The next time you do that, I'm going to turn the airplane upside down and open the door!" And he sat down and shut up and he put his seat belt on, never said a word. He's flown with me a bunch of times after that.

I had this passenger one time, and he was sitting in the copilot's seat, and I was flying and I was taking him to Wainwright or someplace like that. I kept noticing that he kept staring at me. Out of the corner of my eye, I'd see him just looking at me, and I started thinking, "Uh-oh, what's this guy want? What in the world is he doing?" And then he reached over at my temple and plucked a hair out of my head and said, "Look, you've got a gray hair." And I'm sitting there, "Oh, no." That just freaked me out. Anyway, I have a pretty good rapport with the passengers.

If I get stuck in a village, I can walk around and people will come yelling out of their houses, "Ellen, come in and have coffee," or have dinner, or something like that. Even though I live here in Wasilla and I bought a house here, I still consider Barrow my home.

I have had to chase polar bears off the runway before I could land. I would just buzz the heck out of them. Then when you land you sit there and go, "I'm out here, on the ramp, by myself, unloading an airplane, I just chased a polar bear off the runway, where did he go?" You would never believe how fast someone can unload an airplane when they think there is a polar bear right around the corner.

I like to collect rare things. What attracts me to collecting antique airplanes is the research end of it. You're sitting there with this big pile of airplane parts, thinking this is like a puzzle and forty percent of the pieces are missing. Sometimes I have to call all over the countryside for something, and I have to do research on the history of the airplane...like my Fairchild, I know its history from the time it got out of the factory to where it's at now. I know every inch of where that airplane has been.

Out of the ten airplanes I've bought, I bought six of them with no money. The rest of them I've gotten from wheeling and dealing, finagling and horse trading, so to speak. Just the gift of gab—silver tongue. I think if you want something bad enough, you'll get it.

I don't really know of any other Eskimo women pilots. I have flown all over the state, and usually in this business you hear through the grapevine pretty darn quick.

23

LINDA V. HUTTON

Captain, United States Navy *Born October 31, 1951*

Captain Select Lin Hutton, USN, in the doorway of the Grumman C-2A Greyhound. Naval Air Station, Norfolk, Virginia, 1993.

A lot of people say that landing on a carrier is the most fun you can have with your clothes on, and that's pretty close. The first time you go out to a carrier you see how small it is. Lineup is very critical for my aircraft. I cannot drift more than two and a half feet off the center line, because there are aircraft parked on the other side of that landing area, and your wingtip in most cases is only a few feet away. I have the largest aircraft on the carrier to land.

I never thought I would be a Navy pilot. My father was a naval aviator, and everybody around him was a pilot, but that was a very male domain. Women were housewives. They did volunteer work. They hosted formal dinner parties. They advanced their husband's career. And the men went out and flew airplanes.

When I first came in the Navy and received my wings, women could not land on any kind of ship in any kind of airplane. Fixed-wing or helicopter, it didn't matter. You couldn't land anything, for any reason. Then the Navy opened up helicopters, letting women land on ships. The first woman landed on an aircraft carrier in '79, and it's been step-by-step ever since then.

I expected discrimination to exist, and I guess I would have to say I accepted that and tried to just let it roll off my back. Remember, we're talking about 1975. I felt grateful to even have this opportunity. It didn't occur to me that I should feel affronted by the fact that somebody took offense to my even being there. I felt it was perfectly within their rights. I mean, here I was breaking into their domain. I was really viewing it from their perspective. Part of that probably is a function of having grown up as a child of the Navy, and I could understand how all these men could feel this "mucho macho" kind of scenario, and here's this interloper. Who does this person think she is? She doesn't belong here. And so I could understand that. Did

Lin Hutton is the seventh woman to become a U.S. naval aviator and has logged over 385 aircraft landings in a Grumman C-2A Greyhound (also known as the COD). At the time of the interview in 1993, she was the commanding officer of Fleet Logistics Support Squadron Forty, based in Norfolk, Virginia. The squadron flies the Grumman C-2A Greyhound transport carrying supplies and personnel to aircraft carriers in the Atlantic Ocean and the Adriatic and Mediterranean Seas. Hutton was recently promoted to Captain of Major Naval Command in Key West, Florida, becoming the first woman to command a naval air station.

I face discrimination? Yes. But I will have to say I literally ignored a lot of it. I wasn't going to let that distract me, because people can use that to wound you, to shatter your confidence.

Tailhook [a sexual assault scandal arising from a 1991 naval convention in Las Vegas] is a distressing situation. I was looking at the actual DOD-IG report. It's just so frustrating, and I feel sorry in some ways for those guys. What they did was wrong, I really believe that, but the sad thing here is they're also a product of their society, a society that's passing away, that used to think that was acceptable behavior. The old "boys will be boys" attitude. Slowly but surely, as women break into more and more nontraditional fields, that type of behavior is becoming less acceptable. What those guys didn't realize is that times have changed and passed them by.

There's no other airplane more beloved on the carrier than the COD [carrier onboard deliverer]. No fighter guy is going to say, "I love the COD," but I am talking about the five thousand people on the ship—the majority are enlisted people. If you ask them would they rather see the fighter coming back or see the COD land, I guarantee five thousand hands are going to go up for the COD. Why? Because the COD is bringing packages, that letter, that newspaper, magazine, whatever it is. It's their freedom ticket off. The COD is the one that maybe took them off to go home or medevac them if they were ill.

In naval aviation we say angel when we're at a certain altitude. Angels is 1,000 feet. Cherubs is 100 feet. So you say, "I'm at angels 10, descending to cherubs 5," which would be from 10,000 to 500 feet. They'll say, "Mark your father." That means mark your position on my TACAN [tactical air navigation]. We have all kinds of terms. "Texaco" —term for the tanker. If you're out of ammunition, you're "Winchester." If your radar in the nose is out, you're "Lead Nose." That means you just have lead in the nose; it's worthless. "Expect Charlie, five minutes." Charlie means land. "Hawk the deck"—that means watch my deck.

One thing we look for in a successful aviator is good compartmentalization. You've got to have somebody who's got a lot of things going on, but when the chips are down and everything is going wrong in the cockpit, they can compartmentalize. I'm not going to worry about the fact, say, that I'm going through a divorce right now. I'm not going to worry about the fact that my kid is dying of measles. I'm not going to worry about the fact that I've got an electrical problem in the back of the airplane, because right now I've got an engine on fire. It's the ability to put things in the proper department and close the door.

The most exciting thing to me doesn't seem very exciting or sexy, like, "Oh yeah, I made this single-engine landing. People were shooting at me and there I was upside down." No, the most exciting thing for me is getting to work with enlisted people, because they are a cross section of America. They each come with their own agenda, their own goals and aspirations. And the opportunity to work with them is an opportunity to work not just *for* your country but *with* your country.

Captain Select Lin Hutton, USN, seated on an aircraft carrier flight deck. Naval Air Station, Norfolk, Virginia, 1993.

26

FAY GILLIS WELLS

Aviation Pioneer *Born October 15, 1908*

I didn't have any great dream about being anything except having fun and getting through life. Dad said, "You either have to go back to school and get your degree or you have to get a job." I still didn't know what I wanted to do. I was having a wonderful time just living. It just happened that 1929 was the year of the first Women's Transcontinental Air Derby, and Amelia [Earhart] had just flown the ocean the year before [as a passenger], and the papers were full of aviation, and I thought, "Well, I guess aviation is here to stay. Maybe I'd better take up flying." So I went out to Curtiss-Wright and signed up.

I'd only been flying three weeks when I joined the Caterpillar Club. I'd just soloed the day before. They had an experimental aircraft at the airport, and every Sunday they had people doing stunts and things to attract the crowd to come to the airport to take rides. The instructors had been trying to tear this airplane apart to see just how much stress it would take. So it was Sunny's [the flight instructor] turn to fly, and he said, "If you want to go up with me, Fay, I'll teach you some aerobatics." Of course, that was wonderful. Anybody would go up and do that. And so we went up and we were flying around. He was showing all these crazy stunts to me.

At Curtiss Flying Service, everybody had to wear a parachute all the time when you were up in the air. Their instructions were that in case something should happen, you put your hand on the rip cord, step clear of the plane, and then count to ten so you were free from the airplane. That's a very simple instruction. Of course, we were flying upside down, so there was nothing about stepping out of the airplane. The plane just disintegrated. The tail vibrated off, and the wings fluttered and came apart. The vibration knocked the motor off its mount, and apparently my seat belt came loose and I

Fay Gillis Wells seated in front of a photograph taken of her while at Curtiss Flying Service in 1929. Alexandria, Virginia, 1993.

In 1928 Fay Gillis began her career in aviation by jumping from a disabled plane in flight, making her the first woman to join the Caterpillar Club, a group composed of pilots who have made life-saving jumps with silk parachutes. She received her private pilot's license in 1929 and was a founding member of the Ninety-Nines Inc. International Women Pilots. Among other things, Gillis was the first American woman to fly a civil aircraft in Russia, and she worked as a White House correspondent, accompanying President Nixon to China. Today she is cochair of the International Forest of Friendship, a memorial to the world history of aviation and aerospace, in Atchison, Kansas.

fell out. I was thrown out. I was tumbling through the air rolled up in a ball.

Of course, I didn't have my hand on the rip cord, and all those prior instructions, counting to ten, just went out the window. "Where's my rip cord?" I was going crazy. We were flying at about three thousand feet, and they say my parachute opened at about four hundred feet. They saw one chute open. They didn't know whether to wait to bring the pieces in or whether to go out and help shovel me out of the ground or what. But they came out, and fortunately my parachute canopied over a tree, and so I didn't have to worry about breaking my legs or anything else. I was just swinging between two trees up in the branches. Sunny was a bloody mess. Then when they finally got me down, they rushed me right back to the airport and put me in another plane and took me right up. It's like falling off a horse. You get right back on again so you're not afraid. They didn't want to lose a paying customer, you know that. They wanted to be sure I was going to fly again.

I'm so glad that I lived in that era instead of today. It's so much more complicated than when we flew. If [you] wanted to fly, you got in a plane and took off and flew. But now you have half-hour pre-flight check lists before you even get in the plane. We didn't even have starters or brakes. We had to go out and spin our own props, unless we could find some guy who was trying to impress us, who'd come along and spin the prop for us.

The first Ninety-Nines meeting came about because the girls who had been in the first transcontinental air race wanted to stay together, to have some kind of an organization. Amelia [Earhart] came back to New York, and she went to see Mr. Lawrence, who was head of public relations for Curtiss-Wright, and told him this is what the girls wanted to do. Mr. Lawrence had a wonderful secretary by the name of Clara Trenckmann Studer. Clara was a good PR girl, and so she wrote a letter to all the 117 women pilots in America and told them there would be a meeting at the Curtiss hangar on November 2, 1929, and if they were interested, to let us know and to show up.

That morning, I flew out to Hicksville to give a talk to the Boy Scouts, and when I came back, they were getting the workbench ready to put the tea on and the chocolate leaves and a few other things. Everybody was dressed to the nines, and I was the only person in coveralls. Twenty-six girls were there, so they did, indeed, decide they wanted to have an organization. Then we decided on the name. They had this controversy about whether it was going to be the American Association of Women Pilots, or whether it was going to be the Gadflies or the Ladybirds, a frivolous name, and this very calm voice in the background said, "Why don't we name ourselves after our charter members?" It was Amelia Earhart, and that was the first time I knew she was there, because the center of attraction for us at Curtiss was Viola Gentry, who had been up on an endurance flight. They crashed at nighttime in a fog, and the pilot was killed and she spent about six months in the hospital recuperating. We gave her a big bouquet of mums and put her in the front row and everybody fussed over her. Amelia was in the last row. You would have thought Amelia, who was the most famous woman pilot in the world at the time, would have sat in the front row, but that wasn't Amelia. She was very quiet, very reserved, had a wonderful sense of humor, but she never forced herself on any group.

When we decided on that, Clara wrote another letter, which was signed by Amelia and Neva Paris [who worked for Curtiss-Wright]. We said that the number of people that responded to that letter would be the name of our organization. We got ninety-nine responses, and so they were called the Ninety-Nines, and we've been explaining that for sixty-four years. Amelia was made the first president in 1931.

There were four groups that flew through Moscow in 1931 trying to set a record flying around the world. When he [Wiley Post] tried for the record in '33 [the first solo flight around the world], he knew I was in Russia, and so he sent me a telegram and asked if I would help him. I went to the Soviets and told them how much fuel he needed and where, and we needed maps, and all that sort of thing. They didn't have a civilian airline in those days, but they let me fly via the air mail. They put me in, and then they piled the mail sacks over me. That's how I got to Siberia. I waited for him three weeks, because I didn't know when he was coming. He didn't know either, because you'd get held up by weather. He got lost between Moscow and Novosibirsk. We had arranged a place for him to sleep, although he said in his telegram he only wanted to stay two

hours. But I just couldn't believe you could fly all the way from Moscow into Novosibirsk and just refuel and take right off again. I mean, the endurance was incredible. So we arranged for a place for him to sleep, and the Soviets were determined he was going to have a hot meal, and I think three times we took a hot meal out to the airport and he didn't show up. But [finally] he did come and he just stayed two hours.

Wiley was planning another trip to the Far East. He asked me if I'd go, and I said sure. He said he'd like to have me get the visas. Between the time he asked me and the time before his plane was ready, Lint [Wells's boyfriend] had come back to New York and we'd gotten together. It was April 1, 1935, and he and my sister and I were going to the movies that night. Beth said, "Why don't you two get married?" Lint said, "I've asked her for the last time." So I said ask me one more time. I said yes.

I was in Detroit at an air show on the way to go out to meet Wiley, and Lint called me and said, "The *New York Herald-Tribune* wants me to go to Ethiopia to cover the Italo-Ethiopian War from the Abyssinian side," and did I still want to go with Wiley or did I want to have my honeymoon in Africa with him, covering a war. I thought about that for about thirty seconds, and I realized that Wiley could get anybody he wanted to go with him, and I didn't want a substitute on my honeymoon. So I called Wiley, and he was very sweet and understanding, and he got Will Rogers to go with him. They were killed in Alaska, I went to war, and I'm still here.

MARSHA IVINS

Astronaut *Born April 15, 1951*

When the three main engines light, there's a rumble and a shake. After seven seconds, when the main engines come up to speed, the two solid-rocket motors light, and you see the whole period of this vibration increase in amplitude big time—boom—and I mean it shakes! It feels like you've been drop-kicked. If you can imagine the fastest elevator you've ever been in, plus somebody vibrating you, and then multiply that times a big number, that's what it's like.

So in the first four minutes, if something happens you're going to turn around and go back to the Cape. So you think, "I don't want to go back to the Cape. I spent all this time training. Everybody's down there. I'm looking forward to doing this job. Keep going, keep going, keep going." So now four and a half minutes go by, and you can't go back to the Cape. But you could go to Africa. "I don't want to go to Africa. If I go to Africa, I want a good pair of shoes, I want my American Express card, I want a decent set of clothing. I don't have any of that on board. I want to go to orbit. Let's go, let's go." So you're sort of helping the vehicle along all the way.

Now when you finally get to main-engine cutoff, after having been squashed for the past three minutes, as soon as the engines quit—boom—just like that you're weightless. It's almost like a smile happens, because your mouth isn't pulled down and back anymore. You feel everything float. Your books float, your legs float, your arms float. If you took your seat belt off, you'd float out of the seat. For pictures like a crew shot, how do you know that was taken in space? You don't. So I let my hair down, because that's the one indication that there is something not normal going on here. It just sort of hangs out there, and you sort of forget where it is. You can't feel weight, and you get great hairstyles.

When I was fifteen, I started flying airplanes. Today that's not so

....

Marsha Ivins sitting on the launch pad with the space shuttle Discovery *in the background ready for STS-63 (Space Transportation System–63rd Mission). NASA Kennedy Space Center, Cape Canaveral, Florida, 1995.*

Astronaut Marsha Ivins came to the National Aeronautics and Space Administration's Johnson Space Center in Houston, Texas, as an engineer in 1974 and also served as a copilot in the NASA administrative aircraft Gulfstream-1. She applied to the astronaut program three times before being accepted in 1984, and she is a veteran of four space flights. Her current astronaut duties include working as crew support for orbiter launch and landing operations, and she is the representative for orbiter photographic systems and procedures, including the cameras used for IMAX movies. She spends her free time flight instructing in open-cockpit biplanes.

unusual for girls or boys to fly when they're in high school, but back then, kids didn't do that at all. So I was off flying after school instead of hanging out, lying to my parents, and smoking and drinking and doing all the things you're supposed to do in high school. I had an indulgent father who was also interested in flying, so that helped. My mother never liked the idea that my father or I flew airplanes. Her claim to fame was that she had thrown up on every major airline in the world. Air was not her medium. Her mother, on the other hand, used to fly with us in the airplane. She'd sit in the back with her hands folded, with her little pillbox hat on and her purse. My grandmother would say, "You don't understand. When I was born, there were no cars. There were horses and buggies. And now you can get in an airplane and fly where you want. I want to experience that."

I wanted to be an astronaut the first time I saw an astronaut, in 1961. I remember times in school when there was a launch or an EVA [extravehicular activity] and they would bring a little black-and-white TV into the classroom so that you could watch. At the time I thought, "Well, that looks like something I'd like to do." But having it look like something you'd like to do and being able to do it are different things. At the time, astronauts were military test pilots, and I couldn't do that because they weren't taking women. So I looked at what else they were, and they were engineers. I said, "Okay, I'd like to be an engineer." I had decided that if I couldn't be an astronaut, I wanted to work for the space program in any fashion.

Sally Ride was one of the six women chosen, and, no, it didn't change my opinion at all, because it was clear to me from the beginning that they were going to hire men *and* women. So I didn't look at any of them as groundbreakers or someone whose footsteps I would follow in. I've never seen the need to separate men and women as far as what they do, and how they do it. They were going to hire people and I wanted to be one of them.

I believe in the space program, and that's a rarity these days. People believed in the space program we had twenty-five years ago. It's still sort of amazing to me that we can spend so much time talking about the glory of the space program twenty-five years ago and then slam the space program that we currently have. It is still the space program, and the major achievement is to put a person off the planet, whether they go to the moon or they're in low Earth orbit.

If I meet a stranger, I never tell them what I do. I say I work for the government, or sometimes I tell them I own a doughnut shop. If you said to somebody, "Hi, I'm an astronaut," first of all they'd go, "Yeah, and I'm Princess Di," and that sort of thing. But if you start talking and they realize that you're not kidding, you suddenly stop being a person to them. You now become a "what" instead of a "who," and I find that a little distressing.

My trademark is chocolate. I am unintimidated by a recipe that says melt three pounds of chocolate, add a dozen eggs, a quart of cream, and a pound of butter. That doesn't faze me at all. We have even taken

*Marsha Ivins on a launch
pad with external tank and
solid-rocket boosters in
background. NASA Kennedy
Space Center, Cape
Canaveral, Florida, 1994.*

some of my stuff to space. The first time we did it, it was sort of bootlegged. It was on Judy Resnick's [*Challenger* astronaut] first flight, and she was a major chocoholic. So I made a brownie that had no crumbs, because you don't want crumbs in space. We packaged them up in little Zip-loc bags. During the debrief, she said that every morning for breakfast she had a nuclear brownie, and everybody said, "What's a nuclear brownie?" Well, the next thing I know, we had to go public with this.

What is it that keeps me coming back? Space seems to be equally joyful each time you go back. Anybody who's had a dream that they wanted to fly off of a roof and keep going, there you are. When I got into orbit on this last flight, it was like being home. The vehicle tasted right, looked right, felt right.

I don't think it's embarrassing at all to admit, as a person or as a nation or as a planet, that we want to know what's beyond where we can see, or that what we can see, we'd like to see a little closer. For that reason, I think ultimately we will go to Mars and we will visit other planets. I would like to hope we do all the things that the science fiction writers have been writing about for the past thirty or forty years. We colonize and we terraform and we explore. One day technology is going to make it possible to do that quicker, and then it will be, "Why haven't we done this sooner?"

Marsha Ivins stands next to the giant hardware of the external tank and solid-rocket boosters. Ivins refers to the hardware as "something out of Gulliver's Travels." NASA Kennedy Space Center, Cape Canaveral, Florida, 1994.

VICTORIA VAN METER

Student Pilot *Born March 13, 1982*

Vicki Van Meter flew across the country in a Cessna 172 when she was eleven years old and across the Atlantic Ocean the following year in a single-engine Cessna 210. A flight instructor accompanied her for both trips because she did not meet the legal age limit to fly alone. However, she did all of the flying, navigating, takeoffs, and landings without assistance. After the flights she lectured across the country and appeared as a guest on several television programs. *Taking Flight,* her book about her two flights, was published in 1995. She plans to continue with flight lessons until she is eligible to take the private pilot's exam on her seventeenth birthday.

Interview Before Flying Across the Atlantic

I remember the first time I went flying I came back and was so excited. I didn't want to brag or anything, but I felt like I needed to tell someone 'cause my sister was gone [at college] and I couldn't tell her. My brother didn't want to hear it. I went into the other classroom and there was this kid named Kevin sitting in front of me. I said, "Guess what? I just went up in an airplane and it was a really small one and I flew it." And he was like, "Yeah, right. I don't believe you. Yeah, sure, Vicki. Okay. Then you woke up." They didn't believe me, and then finally the teacher said, "Vicki? Why don't you come up here and explain to us what you're doing?" And then they were like, "What?" That was last year, in the fifth grade.

[At ground school] I was with a lot of adults who had jobs, like who were in their thirties or forties, so there was no one close to my age. I went once a week for three hours. We watched the John and Martha King [instructional] videos, and then after that we had a question-and-answer period. They never said, "Why are you in this, you are too young," and stuff. They really didn't mind or anything.

In the summer, when I was getting ready to go across the country, I couldn't reach the pedals and so I had to wear these really big shoes. They were my sister's and so they were really, really, really big. I'd have my regular shoes on and then I'd put them into my sister's shoes and then I'd put them into some other shoes. I looked like a big clown. Luckily, less than a month before I took off, I went up to practice and I could reach the pedals because I had grown a couple of inches.

Well…one point I wanted to make was that when I was going across the country, I didn't have an autopilot so I had to hand-fly it all the way. I liked going over New England because all the trees

Vicki Van Meter standing next to the Cessna 172 in which she flew across the country in 1993. Port Meadville Airport, Meadville, Pennsylvania, 1994.

Vicki Van Meter outside the office of the airport where she learned to fly. Port Meadville Airport, Meadville, Pennsylvania, 1994.

looked like broccoli, like a big piece of broccoli, so that was really neat. Out in Kansas and Missouri it looked like a patchwork quilt—a patch of brown and a patch of green and all that mixed with all the farms and stuff. I got to see the Mississippi flood. I got a better view, and the airport I was going to originally land at was totally underwater, so I had to land at another one.

I never would have thought that I would have been meeting all these people like Hulk Hogan. I got to meet him and he knew who I was. He walked up to me and said, "Hey Vicki! How was the flight?" My brother was really big on WWF [World Wrestling Federation] and all that so we always used to watch it and I never would have thought I'd be meeting him some day so that was neat.

I know I'm young. I was baby-sitting with my friend at a person's house and she [the mother] said, "So, Vicki, you're going to go across the Atlantic, right?" and I said, "Yeah." She said, "In a twin engine, right?" and I said, "No, it's a single engine." She said, "What? Oh my gosh! You can't do that at your age." She wasn't even concerned about the single engine. She was thinking about my age, saying, "I don't think you should do that now, you should wait a couple years." And one of my friends said, "Yeah, Vicki, you should." And I was like, "Well gee, thanks, guys."

There is this big survival suit that you have to have on when you go across the Atlantic. It's this big orange thing and it never sinks and it always floats and I'm like, "Well gee, it's bound to sink sometime," so I went into the swimming pool and I could not turn over—it was really hard to turn over

and swim in. The fingers are only three per hand. It keeps you really warm. Sharks? That sort of thing scares me 'cause I don't really like sharks. I had a bad experience with barracudas. Hopefully, the raft would work and we could climb into that so they wouldn't get us.

I still need some training in the new plane [Cessna 210], but I'm getting used to it and all that because it's a lot heavier when you land. You know, you have to pull back a lot more, but I'm getting used to it. I just got the charts in so I'm just starting to work on them. I'm taking off from there [Maine]. Then I go to Goose Bay, Canada, then to Narsarswaq, Greenland. And I'm stopping over there just for a refueling then from there to Reykjavik, Iceland, and then we haven't decided yet to either fly over the Faeroe Islands or just go straight to Glasgow, Scotland. Then, from there down to London, and then over to France. I'm going to Brussels, Belgium, and then to Frankfurt, Germany, and that's where I'll end it.

I really don't want to set records. I want to do it for the challenge. I don't even know if there's a record to fly across the Atlantic.

Interview After the Trip Across the Atlantic
When I went across the country and we had to make the unexpected fuel stop, I mean, we were able to do that and get fuel. There are little airports everywhere. But going over the ocean, we wouldn't have—we would have just gone down, you know. So it's like, you can take chances over the country if it's thirty-knot headwinds, but you can't over the ocean. Between Goose Bay, Canada, and

Narsarswaq, Greenland, we started to pick up some ice, not a lot of it, just a little of it. So then, after a while, I kept on looking out at the wings, and I was watching the temperature and everything. We started to pick up a lot of ice, and I was like, "Okay, let's try to melt it off," because we were going to have to. So I started to climb out of the clouds and get on the top of them. But then the plane wouldn't climb anymore; I was like, "Wait a minute, the plane's not climbing anymore." The plane couldn't climb because it had picked up so much ice and couldn't operate properly. So then I started to go down to lower altitudes. We were down to 5,000, then 4,000, then 3,000, and so on; then we got down to about 800 feet and we were starting to pop out of the clouds. So then we went down to about 500 feet, over the ocean. And finally, it took a little bit, but the ice melted off. I looked out on the wings and I still saw it was on there. A minute later I looked out and it was all gone. So it was pretty exciting once the problem got solved, because I was seeing the birds fly over the ocean, and the waves and everything.

Well, coming in to Greenland, it was really neat and weird and exciting. When we landed, we weren't expecting anyone, but there were a lot of these kids, these little Inuit kids, that came out to the airport with signs, saying — they were in another language, but you could see [the signs said] "Astronaut Vicki" and stuff. Then I got out of the plane, and they were chanting, "Vicki! Vicki!" So it was really exciting, because we weren't expecting anyone there. All these kids got in a single-file line to come up and get my autograph. They were really, really polite. Then they gave me this shirt and a hat saying "Narsarswaq, Greenland." Not a lot of people must have those, because, I mean, not a lot of people go there.

Well, we carried a GPS with us. That's a global positioning system. What you do, you can program in different things, and it has a moving map on it. It gives you your air speed and exactly where you are, your latitude and longitude, your coordinates, down to the exact pinpoint, so it's pretty neat. At a time if, say, five satellites are working on your antennae or on it, then it will even show you your altitude and stuff. It's really great.

We had nineteen-knot headwinds when we were landing one time in Glasgow. I was happy about that, because the runway was really short. I was used to landing on a two-and-a-half-mile runway with this 210, at Rickenbacker [in Columbus, Ohio], and I was used to sort of taking my time and everything, so when I'd get up to a four-thousand-foot runway, I'd be like, "Ah-oh." I mean, that's a fine runway to land on, but I'd be—not scared, but a little nervous about it. So I was sort of glad that we had that nineteen-knot headwind, so it would slow me down on this short runway.

I'm twelve. So you sort of branch off when you get into junior high. So I think the relationships are changing because of that. It's hard to tell if it's because of what I did or if it's junior high. They like—you know, they treat me different and everything. It's starting to get back to normal, but every day someone still says something about me. I never know when to take people seriously, because

Vicki Van Meter, a few months after flying across the Atlantic, poses at Port Meadville Airport. Meadville, Pennsylvania, 1994.

they're like, "Oh, can I have your autograph?" But they're really teasing me and stuff. And they don't say nice things about me. I mean, there are rumors going around at school that I'm this really big jerk. So I don't know. It's different.

For right now I can't think about flying to anywhere else, to Australia or anything like that, because I have school, and I know that it takes a long, long time to plan out these trips, and it takes a lot of hard practice. I'm getting a lot older now. With this school, I can't miss a week and then go and make it up. I mean, it's a lot harder than that now. So I don't know what an adequate challenge would be. I like tennis a lot and I'm taking that really seriously.

43

MARTY GOPPERT

Flying Circus Pilot *Born April 2, 1941*

In an open cockpit the breeze is hitting you in the face, you're not surrounded by windows or anything. It is just a very delightful free feeling. We have a 1941 Stearman, and when you're flying it, you feel like you're reliving history. It was used at the beginning of World War II as a flight trainer aircraft. The Flying Circus got started by these fellows who had a love of old airplanes. It's a takeoff on the 1930s barnstorming show, placed between Warrenton and Fredericksburg, Virginia, off a country road. We have a grass field, we have an old barn of that era and hangars attached to it where some of the airplanes are stored, and there are seats which are just made out of lumber—nothing fancy by any means, because this is the way it was in the thirties when a group of pilots would fly and give the air show. It's an hour-and-a-half show of aerobatics and little gigs of funniness.

We do a bomb demonstration, we mock it by having one of the members from The Flying Circus out on the runway, looking for his billfold. While he's walking up and down the runway, we have these flour bombs, a package of flour that you cook with, and we try to hit him. And we have a balloon bust where you try to hit a balloon when it goes up in the air with your prop [propeller]. This was part of the precision training used during World War II.

What I enjoy most of all is the ride hopping—being able to take people up, for many of them it's their first time in an open cockpit, and just to see their reactions. We have a little mirror up in the front cockpit so you can see the expressions on the passenger's face. A lot of passengers are not sure whether they want to go or not, and I'll say, "Good afternoon, how are you doing?" and they might get a little grunt out and that's about all. Some of them are scared. They sit down, you get them buckled in, you go up, and you can see by

Marty Goppert dressed in her flying uniform for The Flying Circus, Bealeton, Virginia, 1992.

Marty Goppert is the only woman pilot flying in The Flying Circus in Bealeton, Virginia. Since 1986, she has flown on Sundays, May through October, in an open cockpit PT-17 Stearman. The Flying Circus is operated by a group of volunteer pilots who reenact the barnstorming air shows of the 1930s with antique airplanes. They perform aerobatics and comical stunts, and sell rides (which is known as ride hopping) to the public. After learning to fly at age thirty-eight, Goppert worked for commercial commuter airlines and for a medical airlift. Her other profession is nursing, and she works part-time at George Washington Hospital in Washington, D.C.

Marty Goppert flying an open cockpit PT-17 Stearman in The Flying Circus, Bealeton, Virginia, 1992.

looking up in that little mirror they are really enjoying themselves. These big smiles come out on their faces. I remember I had a little lady who was reluctant to go but her family wanted her to have a ride, and when we got down she said, "You know, it's just like being Peter Pan flying through the air." It's interesting the different responses.

In my early relationship with my husband prior to getting married he took me up and he was doing some loops and aerobatics, and I enjoy them, but that day something had not agreed with me and I got sick. And you have two choices in an open cockpit plane, either you can vomit on yourself or out the side of the aircraft. So of course I chose the better of the two, out the side of the aircraft, and it flew back right into his face, and his goggles were just speckled with my unlucky happening. So we quickly got down. But you know in early love forgiveness comes a lot easier than it would now.

I really never had a great interest in flying. I'm a nurse, and when I would go up with my husband, who was flying for United Airlines, and me being practical and thinking about the whole situation, I wanted

to know how to land this airplane if he ever had a heart attack. You hear about these pilots that become incapacitated and then the person has to land it. So he said, "Well, if you're going to learn to land it, you might as well get your license, because landing is the hardest part."

I got my license so that I could land the aircraft, and from there my love for flying grew. I just really enjoyed going up and flying around and getting away from everything, especially if you've had a hectic day at work, and enjoying the beauty of the country from up above. You don't have the traffic, the hassle, and the busyness of our society that we live in day to day.

The group of people I'm very supportive of and try to encourage are the older women. Part of that is because I didn't learn to fly until I was thirty-eight. Because I was older, there were times when I had to work with myself, especially with landings. It was like, "I'm never going to get this down." You are probably a little more cautious and reluctant, mainly because you're not as adventurous, so you have to work harder at it. If flying is something that you really want to do, and you can get a third-class medical [a physical exam], you can do it. So age is not a factor. You are never too old.

The reason there haven't been other women in The Flying Circus is purely because you have to own an airplane to participate. And I'm just fortunate enough to have a husband who owns one. I'm sure they love to tease me about my landings and so forth, just because I'm the only one out there. I'm always getting ribbed, but that's all right.

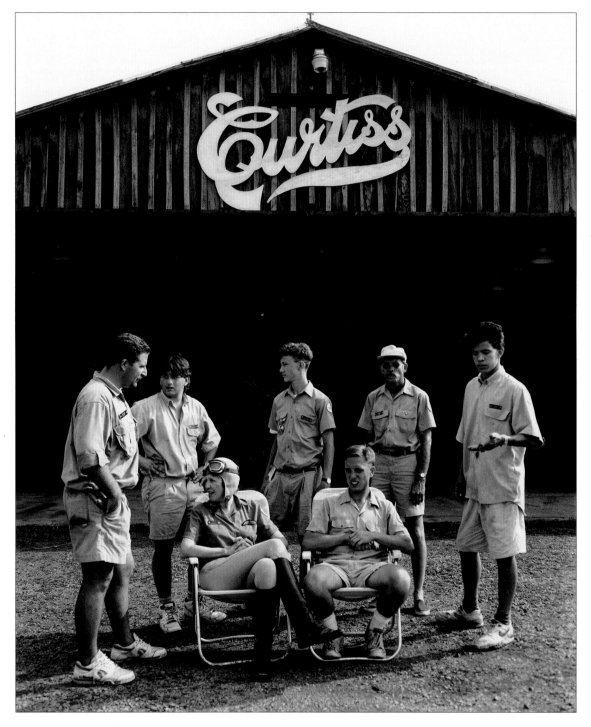

Marty Goppert surrounded by the ground crew at The Flying Circus, Bealeton, Virginia, 1992.

PATRICE CLARKE-WASHINGTON

Captain *Born September 11, 1961*

I think having grown up in a single-parent-family home, where there was no male role model, it wasn't a matter of boys do certain things and girls do certain other things. I suppose if anything, growing up, I always thought if somebody could do it, I could do it, too. I think it was to my advantage, because I didn't have the stereotypes. I've met a lot of people since I've become captain—in particular, black Americans—who have a mind-set that they can't do certain things because they're black. Fortunately, I didn't have that problem.

I wanted to fly airplanes because I wanted to travel and see the world. That's the only focus I've ever had, and that's still the way it is for me. I remember my first day at Embry-Riddle. I was basically in a state of shock. I was pulling into the campus in a taxi. Of course, school hadn't started yet, so there's not a whole lot going on, and it's wintertime and it's gray out. I remember sitting in the back of this taxi, thinking, "What am I doing here?" But anyway, I got enrolled in school and did what I had to do. I still kind of have a sense of just being there and doing what I'm told to do, because an airplane was, from the perspective of flying it, totally foreign to me. I had no idea what I was doing. So [in the beginning] I was in a daze, a state of shock, but doing it, because that's what I wanted to do.

My role as captain is to make sure that all the things necessary to ensure, first, a safe operation, and also an efficient operation are taken care of. Safety always comes first, efficiency second; safety being, one, that the airplane has been checked out. As crew members, we have our different duties to carry out. However, the captain is still ultimately responsible for everything. The hardest part about being a captain is decision time. For a normal, daily operation on an uneventful day, it's a piece of cake. But let's say it's wintertime, the weather's bad, you're going into a station where

Patrice Clarke-Washington in the cockpit of a DC-8, United Parcel Service operation base, Louisville, Kentucky, 1995.

Patrice Clarke-Washington is the only African American woman flying with the rank of captain for a major airline. After graduating from Embry-Riddle Aeronautical University, in Daytona, Florida, she began her career as a pilot for Trans Island Airways and Bahamasair. She later worked as a flight engineer for United Parcel Service and was upgraded to captain in November 1994. Her flying takes her around the world, with frequent stops in Alaska, Hong Kong, Australia, and Honolulu. She is a member of the Organization of Black Airline Pilots.

they're plowing the runways constantly, there's a lot going on, you need to be de-iced. There are a lot of decisions that have to be made all the time, and someone's always going to disagree with your decision. One, I have to make a decision, and once I've made that decision, it has to be a good decision that will stand up not only today, but ten years from now.

In a passenger-carrying operation, there are a lot of frills, from a pilot's point of view, frills that we in the cargo business don't have. For example, when I go to the john in my airplane—or the jane, the toilet—it's not fixed up, it doesn't have a mirror inside; it's just the john; you go there and do what you have to do, and you leave. Whereas in a pas-senger-carrying business, it's all fixed up; they've perfumed it, and so on and so forth, to appeal to the passengers. And you have flight attendants in the passenger-carrying operations. We don't have flight attendants. When we want something to eat, we get up and get it ourselves. The cargo is loaded onto the plane in igloos. I have no idea what's in there.

There is no glamour. It's work. In the pas-senger-carrying business, there's a little bit more glamour associated with your uniform, and there are passengers looking at you, you look good all the time. It's not that we don't want to look neat in our uniforms, but when I get on my airplane, the only other people that look at me are my crew members, and do they care? No. But either side of the fence you're on, I think that glamour is a myth. I really do believe that, because the way I see it is, it's work. It's hard work. You're gone a lot.

I think we all enjoy being gone, but at the same time, it's very taxing to be gone all the time. Not that I'd have it any other way, but there's a price to pay for everything.

The Organization of Black Airline Pilots addresses some of the special needs of black pilots in the industry. The group is small. There are only about six hundred black airline pilots nationwide, at the major airline level. The first woman was not hired by the airlines until 1973. Blacks just got the right to vote, you know, not too many decades ago. It takes time. Not that it's right, not that it's acceptable, but it's just the way it is. Quite frequently blacks are told, no, they can't do it. There are ten or eleven of us, African American females, flying for the major airlines today. Most of the discrimination is extremely subtle. For the most part, I've never had anyone come to me and say, "You are female and/or you are black; therefore, you can't do this. I'm not going to treat you well." But based on my experience and the experiences of other people, I know that I was mistreated. Fortunately for me, I went on about my business and did what I wanted to do.

I started as flight engineer on the DC-8, upgraded to first officer, now captain on the DC-8. For us, as pilots, captain is the top of the line. So I'm a captain, I'm flying a big airplane, one of the bigger airplanes. I have the option of flying to many international destinations, which is what I wanted. I expect another twenty-seven years in the industry, but, yes, I've reached my goal, and UPS did it for me.

....

Patrice Clarke-Washington seated on her flight bag at the United Parcel Service operation base, Louisville, Kentucky, 1995.

51

KRISTA BONINO

First Lieutenant, United States Army, Helicopter Pilot *Born April 18, 1970*

I'm the only female pilot here. To me it's no big deal. When we go out to the field, people sleep in tents. We sleep in our long underwear, especially out here in the freezing cold. You're not going to run around naked or half naked or in little nighties. It gets to the point where everyone smells the same because no one's had a bath, no one's been able to wash their hair, and it's just a matter of people just want to be warm. So no special accommodations [for women] need to be made. My role is the same as any other pilot's role. Whatever mission is handed down, our portion of the mission, nothing is changed because of gender.

Right now I'm working down in D Troop, which is one of the air troops, and I fly the OH-58D Kiowa Warrior. It's a reconnaissance aircraft, and our job is to go find things, look for things. We are like eyes forward. We have a big sight on top, a big ball, and you can see out pretty far with it. We have a TV and also a thermal imager on it, so we can pick up hot spots pretty far away. The S-2, which is the intelligence section, will formulate and plot where we are, what we see, and then kind of come up with an idea of what's going on in the battlefield.

We can hide behind trees and we can still see a few Ks [kilometers] out in front of us. We can do a route recon, just a main road the people are going to be following, make sure there's no one on it, there's not like a tank parked on it or pointing at us. You're just looking for anything, and then you report it back. We are normally deployed forward of the front line. That's where we provide the squadron commander with his information.

It's a blast to fly on the tank trails, because there are a lot of hairpin turns. We have a hundred-degree turn that we have to take, and you get into trying to figure out which way is up. You're taking

1st Lt. Krista Bonino, U.S. Army, holding night-vision goggles needed for flying night missions, Buedingen, Germany, 1995.

Stationed in Germany, 1st Lt. Krista Bonino flies the OH-58D Kiowa Warrior helicopter for the U.S. Army. The Kiowa Warrior is a front-line aircraft used for defensive air combat missions and reconnaissance. Originally from Oklahoma, she was in the Civil Air Patrol as a high school student and is a graduate of the U.S. Military Academy in West Point, New York. She received her flight training at the U.S. Army Aviation Training Center at Fort Rucker, Alabama, graduating in May 1995. The twenty-five-year-old was deployed to Bosnia in December 1995 for the U.S. peacekeeping mission a month after the interview took place.

....

1st Lt. Krista Bonino, U.S. Army, suiting up with flight vest, Buedingen, Germany, 1995.

real high banks, and it's a lot of fun. Our aircraft is very maneuverable, so we can do a lot of that. We don't have as much power as Blackhawks or most of the other aircraft, but we can do the real tight turns.

I think the times that make you catch your breath are when you're flying at night under the goggles [night-vision goggles], because sometimes depending on the moon, the weather, whatever, you can't see that well. Out here, there are wires all over, huge German high-tension wires, and those are scary, especially at night. If you don't know where they're at, they can get you. [The night-vision goggles] amplify the light that comes through—moonlight, starlight, city lights. You see green through them. You

don't see in color, but you can see. They're a real big help when you're flying, because you can see trees, you can see roads, you can see big fields. Your eyes get tired faster. Just the whole night thing, your body is like, "Hey, I'm supposed to be in bed now."

[On Bosnia:] We don't know exactly what's out there. We don't know exactly the weapon systems that they have, what kind of threat there is going to be for us as aviation. Nothing's been finalized. I think sometimes, "Gosh, we might really go," and then I think, "No one's going. We're not going to go." Every day I probably hit the whole gamut of that. It's back and forth.

We fly into different German air bases, we'll shut down and go get lunch or whatever, check weather, and everyone—I mean everyone—looks at me. All the German military guys, and I'll come in and they all do a double take, because they're not used to seeing females around, especially females in military uniforms. So it's really weird when they see me walking around. It's a pretty small community here, real small, so I stick out like a sore thumb.

In '97, I'll be up for captain, and I'd really like to see that happen. Set small goals. I'm a first lieutenant. I really don't think I have enough time in the Army yet to determine whether I want to stay in for twenty years or whether I'd like to do something else. A lot of it depends on where the Army is going and what their needs are, what happens between now and then.

1st Lt. Krista Bonino, U.S. Army, standing on the OH-58D Kiowa Warrior reconnaissance helicopter, Buedingen, Germany, 1995.

LINN BUELL

Glider Pilot *Born November 28, 1945*

"You fly what?" [people say.] Antique gliders. I've flown a Minimoa, from the German Schempp-Hirth factory. That's a rare glider. Most of these gliders were destroyed after the war, but a few survived, having been hidden in barns or moved to Switzerland or someplace. This was a competition glider in the thirties, and it's beautiful. It's a big gull-wing glider, wooden, single-place. It's a real crowd-pleaser, and it's beautiful to watch it fly. Only three women have flown it, and I'm the only one that's not famous. The other two women were Doris Grove, a very well known world-record-holder glider pilot, and Hanna Reitsch, a World War II German test pilot.

In Europe, the vintage glider movement is much larger, and almost every summer I go over there and fly in their meets. I've got to fly lots of different gliders. I've had offers to fly gliders belonging to people I hardly know. I guess they've thought it would be neat to have an American woman fly their glider. There really aren't that many women in the vintage glider movement, I guess because there aren't a whole lot of women glider pilots in general. In Europe, I can think of three other [women] vintage glider pilots that I've met. One's German, one's British, and one's Dutch.

I hope to take my glider, an American glider, over and leave it in Europe for a few years. I don't think they have any Schweizer 1-26s in Europe; I've never seen one. I call my glider Blackbird most of the time. Somebody suggested I should paint a couple of cards on the tail and call it Blackjack, but that doesn't seem to fit it. I think it's more birdlike. We say it creates its own thermals because it generates all this heat. I would never paint a glider black, but its previous owner had done that. Now it causes so much in the way of comments that I'm reluctant to change the paint.

I think in the past gliders were primarily built for men. That's

Linn Buell in the cockpit of a black Schweizer 1-26s antique glider on the airstrip at Scott Air Park, Lovettsville, Virginia, 1995.

Linn Buell has been flying vintage gliders since 1985. She owns a Schweizer 1-26s and Rollanden-Schneider LS4, and has flown in more than forty different types of modern and vintage gliders. Her favorite glider is the Swiss Moswey III, and the rarest glider she has flown is the French Fauvel AV-36 Flying Wing. She participates in the European Vintage Glider Movement, flying in Switzerland, Hungary, the Czech Republic, Germany, and Great Britain. Currently she is president of the Vintage Sailplane Association, with a participation of six hundred members in America and Europe. She is the only female glider pilot at the Scott Air Park in Lovettsville, Virginia.

certainly the case in most of the older ones that I've flown, because I always have to stuff pillows and cushions in to fit. The designers have finally come to their senses in the last fifteen or twenty years, and the rudder pedals and the seats are all adjustable, and the newest glider that I bought has those features, which is really nice.

Being towed in a glider is a lot like formation flying. The beginning of the process is like learning how to ride a bicycle. It's not hard to do, and once you get it, you've got it! Usually problems are caused by turbulence on a real windy day. It can be difficult to maintain position, so during training there are different exercises that we do, like boxing the wake, flying the glider in kind of a square path around the tow plane's wake, an exercise in maintaining position.

Some people have the misconception that gliders are completely quiet and silent, but that's not true. There's wind noise, and that changes with the attitude of the glider in relation to the horizon. Flying gliders can be solitude, a challenge, or scary—or all of these experiences rolled into one flight, which is kind of exciting. It depends on the weather conditions and what your purpose is when you start to fly.

To find lift, I'll tow the glider under the biggest, baddest, blackest cloud I can find. There's always lift there. If I'm in the glider, I'm looking for a cloud that's forming—a cumulus cloud. Thunderstorms have really good lift, but you don't want to get into one of those. There have been gliders that have been sucked up in a thunderstorm.

It's really exciting to get in a thermal and get one centered and then climb several thousand feet. You can see the horizon expand as you go up, and then you can kind of get a visual impression of how far you can go with this one. You have to strap yourself in with your seat belt really tight or you could hit your head on the canopy because of the bumps. The turbulence tends to go away as long as you're working a thermal and flying a circle up in the thermal. When you leave that thermal on a real turbulent and bumpy day, then you'll feel other bumps and other thermals as you're flying from one place to another. But it's not uncomfortable. That's good. When there are lots of thermals, I'm going to be able to stay up for as long as I want.

If I'm flying an event, I'll generally put on a parachute. Years ago there was an endurance record [trial]. It became obvious that it really wasn't an endurance [test] of keeping the glider up, it was about staying awake, because as long as the wind blew against the ridge, you could fly there. I got sleepy once, but at that particular time it might have had something to do with hypoxia, because I was without oxygen and higher than I should have been. Usually flying for long flights, I kind of play games with myself, like if I fly two hours, I can eat my apple.

It's somewhat hazardous landing in a field that's not an airport, because you can't see things that may damage your glider until it's too late. Power lines, of course, can kill you, so you really have to watch for them. I was never concerned for my personal safety, but I was concerned that I would damage the glider. Nobody wants to do that.

Linn Buell standing with her hand on the canopy of a black Schweizer 1-26s antique glider at Scott Air Park, Lovettsville, Virginia, 1995.

I was flying out in Texas, south of Dallas, one time in a borrowed glider on a cross-country flight, and a thunderstorm came up between where I was and the airport that I left. The lift quit, probably because all of the energy was sucked up into that thunderstorm, and I had to land in a farm. It was a real hot day, and I picked one with a pasture near a house and some trees, and when I landed in this field, I realized it was a little too short, so I had to kind of land diagonally across this field. Then there was a hot wire [electric fence] across the corner that I didn't see until I was on the ground, which I took out. That was a hog pen, but the hogs were asleep.

The farmer was startled, and he said, "Girl, are you all right?" He didn't see me land. He turned around and there's a plane sitting in his hog pen. He said not to worry about the hot wire, he'd put that up in about two minutes. Real nice, brought me a Coke and a telephone.

The European guys are very deferential and they're gentlemen. If anything, they go too far with the "Let me do this" attitude. I'm used to assembling gliders and holding wingtips and putting in bolts and stuff, but over there, every time I try to do that, somebody steps in and takes it away from me. I had to force myself not to get angry, but I realized that they're not doing this because they don't think I can; they're doing it because it's the gentlemanly thing to do. That was hard for me to grasp.

Nobody in my family ever flew, except for a cousin of my mother's, and everybody thought she was a little weird. My husband was my very first flight instructor. He always remained pretty neutral. He never encouraged or discouraged me particularly. I've been fortunate that all the flying I've done I've been able to afford, the training and so forth.

When my children were small and my husband was gone a lot, I was training, flying airplanes at the time, and I was working on my commercial instrument airplane ratings. I had to bribe my children with new toys to stay and play in this little square at the airport while I went to take my lessons. Then on instrument flying, since my instructor could only do it nights, I put them in the back of the airplane and off we went. I would have rather not done that.

I have a new toy. In my new glider, I have a computer and a global positioning unit that's really going to be fun. So now when I land in some field other than an airport, I know exactly where I am when I land out, and hopefully it will get me to where I'm going a lot easier.

People have always compared flying to being as free as a bird, kind of trite expressions like that, but maybe it's true. What I think about more than anything else when I'm flying, especially pleasant flights, is "Gee, you know, not very many people get to do this. I'm really lucky compared to the whole world." Very few people get to fly their own airplane or their own glider, and so I'm really grateful that I have that opportunity.

JEAN ROSS HOWARD-PHELAN

Aviation Pioneer *Born September 5, 1916*

There weren't airplanes flying by when I was a kid. Commercial aviation didn't start until the twenties. When [Charles Lindbergh] made his flight [in 1927] and came home to Washington on the battleship *Memphis* and came up the Potomac River, I didn't let him out of my sight. He was entertained at breakfast at six in the morning at the Mayflower Hotel by the National Aeronautic Association (NAA), and my father got invited. I was too young to be allowed to go, so my mother and I sat up in the balcony at the Mayflower ballroom, and I was right over Lindbergh's head and I could watch him eat his grapefruit. And then years later I met him at a reception at the Mayflower that Pan Am [Pan American Airways] gave when he was sort of connected with Pan Am, and we were talking and he said, "What was I doing here at six in the morning?" and I said, "That was the only free moment you had, and the NAA grabbed you." And the poor man. He had just been besieged.

I cut class in high school and took my Christmas money and had my first flight. I went home and told my mother I'd done it. Honest kid. And then when we drove to California one summer when I was sixteen, we were out in Catalina and I had gotten a little unwell on the boat going out, because it's a rough bit of water. I convinced my mother we should fly back in the Sikorsky flying boat.

The war was on, and they started the civilian pilot training program. I got in the last class and learned to fly, and it was the greatest course I ever took. We were our flight instructor's first girls, and he was the youngest pilot in the Navy later. Of course, you always love your flight instructor. That's basic. You always have a "mad feeling" for him.

I gave up an eighteen-hundred-dollar-a-year job in the government, which was dull as dishwater, because I wanted to be in

Jean Ross Howard-Phelan in her home, wrapped in a quilt given to her by members of the Whirly Girls. Washington, D.C., 1993.

Jean Ross Howard-Phelan is the thirteenth woman in the world to receive a helicopter pilot's license. She learned to fly helicopters in 1954, when the president of Bell Aircraft Corporation offered her lessons. Howard-Phelan also founded the Whirly Girls Inc. International Women Helicopter Pilots, now with over a thousand members. She is currently the group's chairman of the board. In 1957, Howard-Phelan was the first woman to be appointed an honorary fellow of the American Helicopter Society. She was an early promoter of heliports at hospitals and helicopters for emergency medical service and crime fighting.

aviation, so I went to Eastern. I loved it, and I wanted to work all the jobs in the airline, and I wanted to be in operations. Captain Eddie Rickenbacker was very tender about his ladies, and he wouldn't let me go into operations. He wouldn't have women stewardesses on the sleeper planes. So I left and got a job with the National Aeronautic Association, which I thought was sort of the overall umbrella of flying events in the country. While I was there, somebody referred me to a wonderful man who was opening a Washington office for Piper, Taylorcraft, and Aeronca. The purpose of it was that an army officer should know how to fly an airplane just as he knew how to drive a jeep. So we sold the first light airplanes to the military. I had the wonderful thing of having an automobile, a downtown parking space, and an airplane, and weekends I would take army guys up and let them fly. I had this happy job, loved it.

Then Miss [Jackie] Cochran came to town recruiting for the WASPs, and I helped her by getting all the Ninety-Nines and women pilots I knew, and we met in her apartment and she gave us the pitch, and I thought I had to go. I signed up, and I had to resign my wonderful job and get on an airplane and go down to Houston, Texas. I started in with the training, but there's a right way, a wrong way, and an Army way, and they didn't like the way I flew, and so I was washed out. Oh, I thought life was over, and my family was so happy. Miss Cochran asked me to stay on and help run the school. Well, I really didn't have the price of a ticket home at that point, so I stayed on. When my class graduated, I just resigned and came home and signed up with the Red Cross and went overseas.

Then I came home. My wonderful boss had moved from his little operation to running the association of all the aircraft manufacturers. It was then called the Aeronautical Chamber of Commerce, and then they changed it to Aircraft Industries. He gave me a job, and that was just super, and I stayed there forty-one years, first with the small plane division. I promoted the thought that the manufacturers would lend us an airplane so I could help promote aviation, because I felt that no husband could buy an airplane if his wife didn't want him to. So I concentrated on taking women up for their first flights, the heads of women's organizations and stuff, around Washington. Some of them, I think, enjoyed the jeep ride out to the airplane at National Airport more than the flight. They always wanted to fly over their house, and then I'd take a picture of them by the airplane and send it to them later.

But then I got transferred to helicopters. I helped with this show down in Maryland, when they were demonstrating helicopters to the National Association of State Aviation Officials. Looking back, I think it probably was the first air show of helicopters, and I had my first flight in a helicopter, just a little hop, and I thought, "This is for me." So I kept dropping hints to our company presidents, and I said I'd do a better job if I knew how to fly them. Larry Bell, president of Bell Aircraft, said, "Get yourself to Fort Worth and we'll teach you." This took about seven years to get them to say that.

I was the first girl down there they'd ever had. My instructor, who was, of course, the greatest, had never had a woman student. Anyway, he said to hover—that's when you're parked in the air—he said it's like baking a cake. Well, he obviously had never baked a cake. I'm doing a square dance all over the place. Actually, it's just the lightest touch on all the controls, really. So it took me a while to learn to hover. I thought I'd never learn. But I finally did and passed my test and got my rating.

Almost immediately I wondered how many other women there were, and I started writing to manufacturers and aero clubs here and abroad. I thought I was the eighth wonder of the world, and then I found out that there were twelve of us and I was number thirteen. Then I wrote them and invited them to come to Washington so that we'd meet and organize, and they all responded.

Seven came and the others sent word that they approved the idea, which was great. I had a nice friend at Bell who wrote the letter for me in German to Hanna Reitsch, the first in the world, and then Stanley Hiller, president of Hiller Helicopters, contacted General Valerie André. She wasn't a general then. She was the first one in France, and she was the brain surgeon and the parachutist and everything else. And so she agreed. So we got them all, and that's how the Whirly Girls started.

The first day we met, we said we were going to give scholarships. That was one of our reasons for being, we felt, to help other women get into helicopters. We assign numbers according to when you get your rating. Their numbers are kind of a status symbol. (Kids used to call me at the office and say, "This is 119," or, "This is 378," and I'm supposed to know who they are. And I did for a while.) At our annual "hovering" [Whirly Girl meeting], we have a very brief business meeting and then each girl is asked to stand up, give her name and Whirly Girl number, and then tell what they've done during the year, and it's mind-boggling what they do.

Joyce Failing, Whirly Girl 145, I think, suggested for them to give me that [quilt], which was overwhelming. They wrote to each Whirly Girl and sent her a white square of muslin and black thread and said, "Embroider your name, number, and country." And some of them panicked. Some of them wrote and said, "I'd rather hover in a crosswind than embroider," so quite a few had it done professionally. Then at a hovering, I didn't know anything, and they suddenly walked down the aisle carrying this quilt and presented it.

I don't think everybody wants to fly. But I think it opens a whole new everything for you, socially and careerwise. Now the careers are super. I think as Jackie Cochran said, that everything good in her life had come about because of aviation, and I can certainly say that.

MARY EDNA FRASER

Aerial Artist *Born March 20, 1952*

I was flying from the time I was two weeks old. At least once a month, we would go to my grandmother's in Candor, North Carolina. That was about an hour flight. There were four children, so Daddy would buckle two of us into the Ercoupe. My sisters and I would be dressed up in our Sunday dresses and little white socks and patent leather shoes. We'd get there just before church, and buzz Grandmother's house and she'd pick us up.

I adore getting in an airplane. Before I climb up into it, my adrenaline starts. I love the smell of the airplane. The Ercoupe is a real unique kind of airplane. It's a low-winged plane, and it's very, very tiny and very, very slow. The cockpit opens, so you slide it down and it's like a bubble top. Sometimes when I'm photographing, I'm getting the wind in my face, but you have a clear view of whatever you see. It's a wonderful way to fly, because you feel so birdlike.

I had been a batik artist for two or three years, and my brother took me flying over the Sea Islands of Georgia. There are so many little islands in that area, and the marshes made such gorgeous designs. I saw the designs and the change in patterns just by moving the plane up the coast. I then realized that I would never get bored with that viewpoint.

It's kind of crazy, because the batik process is already slow and tedious in a way, and I'm adding another part to that. I think the aerial point of view lends itself to cloth. When you're in an airplane and you're looking, the atmosphere of the air is pretty easy to put into cloth, with the sheen of cloth, and the way that silks can be hung in the air. Even though it's an ancient craft, it has so much to be explored, so many ways to push it beyond the levels it's been dealt with in the past.

Mary Edna Fraser in the cockpit of her grandfather's 1946 Ercoupe, Charleston, South Carolina, 1993.

Mary Edna Fraser uses aerial landscape photographs as the foundation for her artwork. These photographs are transformed into designs for large-scale batiks (an ancient art process using dye and wax on cloth). Exhibited and collected around the world, her batiks have a common theme: promoting the awareness of environmental beauty and change on the planet as seen from the air. Her most recent project is titled *Silken Tableaus: Earth and Planetscapes in 2003,* which will portray the geographic wonders of the earth and solar system using her images combined with satellite data images. The artist resides with her husband and two daughters.

Mary Edna Fraser working on a batik in her studio, Charleston, South Carolina, 1993.

Being a visual person, flying—especially over undeveloped land areas I can see everything—puts life into perspective. You're just a little tiny piece of that world. My own spiritual beliefs are enhanced by seeing this round curve of the earth's horizon and how much has been created and how beautiful and perfect it is. But another part of flying for me is that I've seen what man has done to the earth. Other people don't see the great big holes [left by] mining. Whenever [my brother] Burke and I were flying up the coast, I thought I'd get shots all the way up Florida back to South Carolina, and I didn't, because man has altered the water so much that it's no longer a natural curving beautiful thing. It's these little strange brick areas, little rectangles all the way up. So you can really see which states have taken care of their land and which ones have allowed development to take over.

When I first started flying, I was just taking pictures, just straight out having fun. You're getting ready to go somewhere that you've never seen, and you don't know what you're going to see because it isn't your space. Then I realized people wanted to know what these pictures were of, what bay, what body of water. So before I go—for instance, before I went to shoot the Rio Grande and Georgia O'Keeffe's part of the world—I study maps. If I'm on the coast, I usually study nautical charts, because that way I know what is going to be fascinating from the air. Then I can see, flying around it, which angle I'm going to want to come to, and I can tell by the size of it whether to fly at a high altitude or a low altitude. So it saves money and time.

Whenever I go someplace, say Maine, I try to camp out and explore the area from the ground and from the air to get a sense of place, and do little paintings on the ground. I found that color in nature is very brilliant. I'll run outside and match a sky or match the marsh, or I'll pick up things and take them into the studio for color reference. I can make my dyes match the flowers and the flora and the fauna. I'll bring into the studio, into my dye room, little samples of color that I think would be beautiful together. So I can take those colors and put them into my work by using color theory, pump them up a little bit more by putting them next to other colors. They may not be believable, but they are real, because I got them right off of a source.

I've been focusing on the United States primarily. I would like to do some more designs of the earth from a larger focus. I've shot a little bit of France and some of Iceland. With satellite images, I can see a lot of places that I'd really like to get above and photograph. I'd love to shoot the Himalayas and the Alps. I'd like to shoot Puget Sound and Alaska. I'd really like to fly over Hawaii myself. I think deserts would be pretty fascinating from the air. I want to do Indonesia really bad and New Zealand.

There's an excitement and a form of peace in the air. You don't have any of the pressures of life around you. It's sort of an escape into another realm.

MAYTE GRECO

Search and Rescue Pilot *Born October 8, 1959*

[Author's Note: The interview with Mayte Greco took place on February 23, 1996, the day before two Brothers to the Rescue planes were shot down by the Cuban military, killing the crew members.]

Once we became a real group, we had to come up with a name. We wanted a name that would show Cuba in a sense that we were their brothers, that we wanted to help them. I remember everybody turning around and looking at me. "Brothers. That doesn't mean that you're not included." I was like, "It's okay. I know brothers is a universal thing." I didn't care what we were called; I was going to go anyway.

We fly out of Opa-locka, Miami, Florida, and we head on southwest. We have a search pattern that's in between the Florida Straits and Cuba. We usually go with three airplanes. There is always a mission commander, and that person tells you what we're going to do for the day or what the search area is going to be, who's who. We've never left without holding hands and saying a prayer. We pray for the rafters out there, we pray for us, and we'll pray for our eyes to be sharp to look out there, and then we go.

We fly at about five hundred feet, and when there's a raft we come down low, very low, to see what kind of a boat, how many people, their condition, and eventually throw water. These people have been coming for over thirty-five years, just Russian roulette, see if they make it or not. We've got babies, women, children, we have criminals, we have professionals. They're willing to risk their lives for a real life.

The traditional raft is an inner tube and a person in it. They kind of keep adding on to that theory. We've seen like ten inner tubes put together. There once was a bus that had the top cut off, and that was

Mayte Greco standing among rafts that Cuban exiles floated on to leave their country. Opa-locka Airport, Miami, 1996.

Cuban American Mayte Greco is a founding member of Brothers to the Rescue (Hermanos al Rescate), an organization of pilots whose mission is to fly search and rescue operations over the ocean between Florida and Cuba searching for Cuban exiles in rafts. Her job as the pilot is to spot the tiny rafts from the air, notify the Coast Guard, and drop food and water to the passengers. She then circles the raft until the U.S. Coast Guard comes to their rescue. The thirty-six-year-old mother of five children also owns and flies for Wings Air Charter, an air taxi service operating from Fort Lauderdale, Florida, to Great Harbor Island, Bahamas.

Mayte Greco sitting in cockpit of a Brothers to the Rescue Cessna, Opa-locka Airport, Miami, 1996. This plane was shot down the following day, killing the crew members aboard.

thrown in the water, and they just sat on that. Styrofoam—that's been a biggie, big pieces of Styrofoam that refrigerators were in or something—they'll get that and just sit on it and float. He carries maybe water tied to something on him, he usually wears a hat, and off he goes and hopes for the best.

The main thing that we drop from the airplane is going to be water. These people are really dehydrated, so that's really the one thing. We've gotten a lot of donations, leftovers from the Gulf War, of MREs, the ready-to-eat meals, and we drop that, too, so they can have something to eat. It's never enough, the water that you give them. I mean, they'll drink and drink, and they want to pour it over their face. You can see they're in real need of this water.

The idea is to get as close to the raft as you can and drop it right next to the raft so they can reach and pull it out. We don't want to hit the raft, because these rafts are usually in very poor condition and we can make a hole in them.

We don't want them swimming for anything. They'll jump immediately. There was a young boy in a raft and he went out after the water. A shark followed him straight to the raft. We were in the airplane, there was nothing we could do, and we were just waiting for this shark to grab this kid, but he got lucky and he made it back in the raft. It was eight hours before these people got picked up.

Depending on the airplane that we fly, on the average we have six hours of fuel out there. There are some days that are so hot. We don't have air-conditioning in the planes.

You don't want to drink water because you know the rafters don't have water, and if you drink water, then you've got to think, then I have to go to the bathroom. When we feel like it's a good day or we know there are rafts, it keeps you going, so you take just a few feet at a time and you're looking and looking, and days when there's no action, we can feel that it's very long. You're sitting cramped up in a very small place with no ventilation.

We see more empty rafts than rafts with people on them, so we know that a lot of them have not made it, and that's really sad. That makes you think, "Had I been here four hours before, would we have been able to help him? Did he just die?" Every time we see a raft, it's a very emotional moment for everyone, not just the one that sees it, but all the airplanes that are out there.

Many times, we see sharks. It's usually very common when the people have been in the boat for a long time. Most of them put their feet in the water, to cool off, so they keep their feet in there. Their feet rot, and this must be attracting the sharks. I think the sharks can sense that there's somebody decaying already, and they'll circle.

What do we see? [Here's an example.] It's a sinking raft. The guys have water inside, a lot of water. Their legs are covered with water. There are sharks, two sharks right by them. So we go ahead and call a Mayday. The Coast Guard is close by. There are rocks, so the Coast Guard has to make a wide turn to come in. They start coming in. The raft is sinking more. They've got water now to their chest, and they're just begging for help, and really they're desperate. So my pilot and I, we looked at each other and we didn't see any option but to take off our life jackets and throw them at them. We both looked and said, "This is all we've got. If we go down, this is all we've got." And we looked, and without any hesitation, off went the life jackets and we threw them at them.

You always have immaculate windows on your plane, because you want to see very well. So I'm always cleaning windows. I was really the only girl flying for probably a couple of years, and I would get a little upset at times, because people from the outside, reporters, somehow assumed that I was the window washer and never even assumed that I was one of the group, that a lady was going to be going out flying.

A very exciting moment for me was when I first got to see Cuba. We fly pretty much the whole length of Cuba, and you see the buildings, you see Havana, you see the mountains. I know that I've been Cuban all my life, people ask me, "Where are you from?" and I say, "Cuba." But I never felt Cuban till the first day that I saw Cuba.

If we invade their air space, we're in big danger. We've been threatened. I was there once when they sent out a MiG, and it was very interesting because the thing just zoomed really close to the airplane. Our transponder was lit. We had definitely been intercepted, and we just said, "Okay, it's time to head on back home," and kind of took a turn and hoped that nothing would happen.

I said a little prayer, because if they have bad intentions, we're nothing. That was an early flight. We think they're not out there anymore because we don't think they have

money for fuel. We don't think they're going to be throwing MiGs at us.

I have so much fun with my flying, and I love it. To me, it's almost as wonderful as a little smile on a baby. I knew that I wanted to fly airplanes since I was about six years old. But being from a Latin background, it was not a very typical female thing to do. You were supposed to grow up and have babies.

My parents didn't know I was taking flying lessons. It was my secret; nobody knew about it. I was doing my flying lesson, I was doing some touch-and-goes, and when I came in for a landing, I see this person on the runway, and I was like, "Oh, there's a nut out there, a worker or something!" So I go around, I come back again, and that person was still there. I was a little concerned at this point. I had a bad feeling about the whole thing. "What's going on?" So I go around again. When I came back the third time, I realized it was my father.

I started college and I met my husband. I got pregnant, and immediately everybody said, "Oh, you can't fly when you're pregnant." I was nineteen and kind of believed it, and I didn't. Then I had another baby and another baby and another baby, and it was hard for me to go fly, but I don't think a day went by that I didn't think of getting back in the air. When I put my fourth daughter into preschool, I knew what I was going to do, so I headed out to the airport and that's when I got my license.

We were going down the chain of Elbow Key, a beautiful chain of rocks, belonging to the Bahamians. A lot of Cubans see these rocks in the distance, and it's a pretty safe

Mayte Greco with her five children at Opa-locka Airport, Miami, 1996.

refuge for them if they hit it on the right side. So we always patrol that area. I took a quick look off to the side, and I spotted a little boat. So we went ahead and went over, and as we were getting close to it, we see that they're waving something, and it was a baby.

Having children and being on boats out here in Florida in the summertime, knowing what it is to be on a boat, I felt so happy that we were there. It was very emotional. We didn't know what to give them. We were trying to think, "We've got to do something extra for the baby. Babies aren't so resistant to all that weather and the sun and stuff." So I remember immediately calling the Coast Guard and telling them, "We've got a baby on board. We've got a baby on board," and

because there was a baby on board, I think that was probably one of the quickest ones that we ever had rescued. I made it a point to get in touch with [the rafters] afterward. I was angry, I think, that they had a baby on board.

Something very hard to do on a mission is to head home, especially if you still have an hour of fuel. It's very hard turning back in. As you start approaching the shore, it's like a feeling of, "They're out there alone."

When I see these people, what they're expressing, their emotions, it's like you've given them a new life. You can see that from the air. I've met some of these rafters that come, I follow up, and they really go out and pursue their dream. Maybe we did make a difference in their lives.

FLORENCE PARLETT

Airport Operator *Born December 16, 1905*

I admired the barnstormers that used to come around at the county fairs. I would love to go see them. They'd always ask, "Does anybody want to go for a ride?" I always wanted to go, but Mama said, "No, No, No, No, No." Mama wouldn't let me go up because it was too dangerous, and for a long time my husband wouldn't let me go, so we kind of tricked him into it. My oldest son said, "Dad, I'm gonna give Mama an airplane ride for Mother's Day." And he couldn't quite say no to it. And that's how I got my first ride, in 1947. Then he was teaching me how to fly and all, but he said, "Mama, I can't solo you unless Daddy says so." So my husband gave up. He thought I may as well have it, so he went ahead and let me get my license.

My two older sons had the airplane and when they got married they didn't want to have their money tied up in the airplane, they wanted a house. So my husband and I bought the airplane and that's how we got started. I said, well we got an airplane I ought to learn how to fly this thing. People would say, "Act your age, old lady!" I heard it hundreds of times. "You're too old to be doing that, Florence."

Mr. Lee had the airport here, and it was just a little open field, and they had people who just went broke all the time. I belonged to the Civil Air Patrol and we thought we would have an open house, so I went to Mr. Lee to ask him, and he said, "Well, the airport is in such bad shape…" It was closed at the time. So I said, "Well, I'll fix it up, and get the ruts out." And so Mr. Lee said, "Well, you go ahead and take over the airport," and we did it on a handshake.

My husband didn't want anything to do with the airport. It was definitely understood that this was my problem, and everything up here I had to take care of, although I could use his truck, but I couldn't depend on any help out of him. I didn't have any money to do much with, but I had a lot of energy. You learn as you go, you

Florence Parlett standing in front of a hangar at Lee Airport, Edgewater, Maryland, 1993.

Florence Parlett actively flew until she was eighty-three years old. Since 1956 she has operated Annapolis Flying Service at Lee Airport in Edgewater, Maryland. The business provides airplane rentals, flight instruction, and fuel. An avid promoter of aviation education, she has taken many school groups for tours of the airport. In 1987, zoning regulations threatened to close the airport, but she fought back by throwing an open house, giving free rides to the public, and winning their vote to keep the airport open. She has been honored by the National Aviation Club and the Federal Aviation Administration as an outstanding pioneer.

keep an open mind, and you always got something you can put in it.

I gave a lot of rides. Anybody who comes through this door says, "Remember way back in 1960 or 1970 you gave me my first ride?" They're always coming in and telling me that. I had to get my commercial license so I could give rides, so I had to go up and get that, and it wasn't easy for me because I got airsick a little bit. You do those lazy eights, they kind of swirl you around a little bit, and I would get quite oozie with it.

To really fly and enjoy things there's nothing like the old Piper J-3. It's just like flying a kite almost, yet it's not very forgiving when you try to make a landing. I used to get the cadets [midshipmen] from the Naval Academy to come out here, and they see that little ol' plane and it looks so simple. They would want a checkout ride so then they can fly it. When you get it on the ground, that's really when you have to work on 'em, because that plane would skid around on you and go every which way. And besides that we had mud holes, just a pothole here and there, and I'd say, "Watch that," and [one midshipman] said, "Mrs. Parlett, you're trying to get me to fly this airplane on this field, and I couldn't even play football on it." About that time he hit one mud puddle and it went all over him—but he didn't sue me.

This one little kid who wanted a ride and didn't have any money said, "Mrs. Parlett, if you take me for a ride I'll bring the money later on." I took the little ol' J-3 I had and took him up for a ride. He didn't say a thing through the whole ride. I got down, he got out and said, "Oh, there is nothing to that, all you do is wiggle the stick!" That's what you control it with, you know, he didn't see my feet working on the bottom. He never did come back and pay me.

In 1978 we worked on a movie, [*The Seduction of Joe Tynan*], here at the airport, with Alan Alda and Meryl Streep. They wanted to put some flying into it. I had to teach Ms. Streep how to start the airplane so she could taxi it around a little bit, and then I would take over the controls and do the flying. I had the same pair of gloves that she had on, and when she was taxiing around I got in the back and lay down behind the seats. She was very good at learning, but it was my airplane and I fly it. Whenever the key went out, I went with it.

I wasn't out there to just fly, I was out there to promote aviation. And what I tried to do ever since I've been here at this airport is to keep my prices down so that the ordinary people could afford it. I've kept my overhead down to a very sheer minimum to be able to give that to the public.

I had four boys but the oldest, Buddy [Leonard H. Parlett, Jr.], who taught me to fly, was killed in an accident—and I lost him. He took off from here but he crashed about six miles away. We knew very well that he would have wanted us to keep on.

I'm up here every day. I do the books for the airport and pay all the bills. I make the judgments on everything. The responsibilities and the decisions are mine to make, and if things go wrong, they're still mine.

Florence Parlett holding shirttails from former students who soloed at Lee Airport, Edgewater, Maryland, 1993.

SHANNON LUCID

Astronaut *Born January 14, 1943*

When I was about five years old we were leaving Shanghai, China, in a converted Army DC-3. My sister and my brother were real sick, and the doctor said they had to get out of Shanghai for the summer. We got in, we took off, and then we climbed up, and we were going over the Guilin Mountains. It wasn't pressurized, and my brother got sick and my sister was sick and my mother was turning green. I was looking out the window, and I thought this was the most wonderful thing I'd ever seen in my entire life. Then as we were coming in to land, I remember seeing a guy down there, he had a red scarf around his neck, and I thought, "Wow, here we are, and some human being is flying this airplane and we're going to land on that small strip down there." I thought that was the most amazing thing that a person could ever do, and so right then and there I thought, "As soon as I grow up, I'm going to learn how to fly."

When I was in college, I worked not only to go through college, but to save up for flying lessons. I was making fifty cents an hour at one of my jobs, and my flying lessons were costing me ten dollars an hour. I had several jobs where I cleaned houses for people; I would be their maid, essentially.

I got my license, and what I really wanted to do was to fly for a living. I had a chemistry major at that time, so I thought I'd use my chemistry to get a job to finance my flying. I asked my professors, I said, "I'm getting out. How do I go about getting a job?" because I didn't know anybody who worked as a chemist. They just looked at me and said, "Shannon, no one's going to hire a female chemist." But I finally did get a job, and so I used all my money and I bought an airplane.

Ever since I was a little girl, and obviously that was a long time before there was such a thing as a space program, I read all the

Shannon Lucid, Ph.D., was selected into the astronaut program with the original core of women astronauts in 1978. At the time she was married and a mother of three children. A veteran of four space flights as a mission specialist, she spent her fifth flight (*Atlantis* STS-76, March 1996), spending approximately 188 days in space on board the Russian space station *Mir*, conducting research with two Russian cosmonauts. She is the first American woman to live aboard *Mir* and holds the record for the longest time in space for an American. Lucid graduated from the University of Oklahoma with a background in biochemistry and is a commercial, instrument, and multiengine rated pilot.

books I could find on rockets and talked to everybody that I knew about it, and no one, of course, cared to listen.

When [NASA] started up the space program, you know, you felt disenfranchised, because it was all males and there were no females. I can remember I wrote a letter to *Time* magazine as soon as they selected the original seven Mercury astronauts and said, "Why are there no females in this group?" So they wrote back and said that it wasn't suitable or something. But anyway, I was very interested in the program, and as soon as they came out and said that they were going to make another selection and have females included in the group, I sent my application in. I think my application must have been in the first forty that came in.

I had three kids when I came into the program. I think because of the way our society is structured, a lot of women sometimes feel a little guilty if they work. Obviously, when I was raising [the children] in the sixties and the early part of the seventies, it was not looked on favorably for a woman to work, especially if she had children. So you had to justify in your own mind why you were going against the norm. I took all the kids flying by the time they were a week old so that they knew that they were living with me and I wasn't living with them.

[Living aboard the shuttle is] just like being in a camper when it's raining outside and you can't let your kids out and no one can go anywhere. [But] it works out real well. I've always had a real good time. The thing that I think is amazing is how much housekeeping you have to do to keep stuff picked up. I just don't think that people down here realize how much time is spent picking up trash and making sure you know where everything is.

Now if your flight is over ten days, then midway during the flight your family can come in and have a few minutes where they can talk privately, in a conference call. So they were able to do that on the last flight I was on, and they thought that was pretty neat. My son told me that he had just gotten his midterm grades and he'd gotten a job, and my daughter was telling me about her car trouble.

[The *Challenger* accident] made a big impact on everybody, obviously, because you lost your friends, and it made an impact on your kids also. I know my oldest daughter was in high school at the time, and her comment was that she thought that astronauts were the most selfish people in the entire world, because they would do a job that would put them at risk. Anytime something happens, you can look back in hindsight and say, "If this had been done, then it wouldn't have happened," so there was a lot of that, too.

We're going to be building a space station at some point in the future, and we haven't had any experience with that since the Skylab days. We're launching in March for about a hundred and forty days [to live aboard the Russian space station *Mir*]. I think it's a lot better for Americans and Russians to be working together rather than against each other.

Shannon Lucid in Russian-language class under photographs of former cosmonauts at the Yuri Gargarin Cosmonauts Training Center, Star City, Russia, 1995.

LORI LOVE

Crop Duster *Born May 10, 1950*

When I was five, I figured out that girls could fly airplanes too. I don't know how I came to that conclusion. We never had a television. We lived twenty miles from the big Wichita International Airport. My parents would stop there at night because all of the blue taxiway lights looked really pretty. That's about the only thing I remember about flying. I started skydiving and flying when I was in college.

For some reason still unknown to me, I stopped by a crop dusting school in Arizona and ended up teaching crop dusting there before I ever had any experience. It was some strange combination of their need for an instructor, and I came along, or maybe it had something to do with there was some conflict going on between the guy who owned the place and the chief pilot, and I think maybe one of them thought that I would screw the job up. I could already fly a tail-dragger. I would give one lesson and then come running back to the guy to see what I was supposed to do the next time, he would explain it to me, and I'd go do the next one. I taught myself a lot in the first couple of months. Well, I pissed a lot of people off. I don't think they thought I would pull it off, and I did. So it turned into quite a flourishing school for a number of years. That's where I started. I stayed out there for quite a while—six or seven years.

[In] crop dusting, [it] is pilot error, generally, when people get killed. A very good friend of mine got killed here last year. Off the top of my head, I was going to say it didn't affect my flying, but every time I see those big power lines—every crop duster knows if you hit those giant ones with the steel towers, you're going to die. Power lines are probably the biggest danger because they are always in the way and you have to either go over them or under them. We go under them a lot. I've gone through several power lines. Most of the time [when] you hit a power line, you cut it and go right on. Well,

Lori Love standing in front of a Turbine Ag Cat at Onstott's crop dusting hangar in Yuba City, California, 1995.

Crop duster Lori Love travels around the country in her van, spraying chemicals or fertilizers on crops from different aircraft. Flying six to eight feet off the ground, she covers rice, cotton, forestry, orchards, and corn. Her daredevil stories of dodging power lines are hair-raising, but the pilot has over twenty years of flying and an impressive list of ratings to prove her expertise. She also flies helicopters, gliders, and hang gliders. She has also ferried planes to Europe and Central and South America. In the winter months she can be found in Florida at a drop zone, instructing sky diving.

actually, I got tangled up in one once. It stretched and stretched and stretched, and finally broke. One end of it wrapped around the horizontal stabilizer and the elevator and crumpled it up into a little ball. The other end wrapped around the rudder and vertical stabilizer and ripped off the top half of the rudder, at which point the airplane started flying really funny. I didn't know what had happened, but I decided I should land it. Unfortunately, that was in a very wet cotton field but I landed it just fine, and as it slowed down and the wheels sank in, it turned over on its back, which didn't hurt me, but it wasn't very good for the airplane.

Good spray coverage is six to eight feet off the ground. I have trouble around here because in so many parts of the country they want the wheels down in the crop, which is not your best spray coverage, but the farmers are convinced that's the best spray coverage. I have a habit of running the wheels down through the stuff and Charlie's always out there, "Up, up, go up higher." "Okay, I forgot again."

If you're flying some crop like cotton that's big and leafy and you get down too low, it grabs the wheels and doesn't want to let you back out again. There's not really much danger of flying into the ground.

The best work is on the West Coast because it has the longest seasons. There are seasons all the way across the country. The rice season is different because we can fly in all sorts of weather, because it's dry materials — fertilizer and rice seed and whatnot. We go to work at five o'clock in the morning. We get everything set. The crews go out to the strips. We get the flaggers to the field. We take the airplane out to the strip and get a load and go put it on the field. Get a load, go put it on the field. But here, because of the dry stuff, we can fly in wind like we have now, which is thirty miles an hour. We can fly in pouring rain. We fly in all weather conditions all day long and just keep going. So that's one good thing about the rice season, you can just keep flying. I haven't done tomatoes, potatoes, and onions. That's coming up this year. Lots of cotton, corn, lots of rice. What else do we have around here? Beans, peas, just about everything you can think of, actually. Wheat, sugar beets. I haven't done sugarcane. That's down in southern Florida. I mean, everything gets sprayed now and then.

With some regularity, people don't believe that it's actually a female in the airplane. Once many years ago I was out at some small strip in Arizona loading the airplane myself, because it was a very small job, and the grower drove up, looked around, and said, "Where's the pilot?" I said, "I'm the pilot." He looked around some more and says, "Well, when the pilot comes back, would you tell him so and so?" I said, "Okay, I will," and he drove off.

I get really bored not being on the road. I had my own airport in Alabama for five years, and I signed a five-year lease, and at the end of the five years, I couldn't wait to go somewhere. I don't have a house. I have a Dodge Maxivan, and everything I own is inside it. I honestly thought by now I would be tired of that lifestyle and be ready to settle down, but it hasn't happened.

Lori Love flying Ag Cat over rice fields in Yuba City with a "flagger" in foreground. Yuba City, California, 1995.

MADGE RUTHERFORD MINTON

Women Airforce Service Pilot (WASP) *Born March 22, 1920*

My parents were always saying, "Control yourself Madge, control yourself." The first really strong wish as to the future came to me the first time I saw an airplane. I was sitting on the curb eating a piece of my grandmother's pie and this little plane was up maybe a couple or three thousand feet. It looked like a toy. I went in and I said, "Mother, there's something up there and I want you to get it for me so I can play with it." It landed in a pasture not far from us, and when we got there, there was this open-cockpit biplane and your typical pilot in the hot pilot's scarf and the goggles, and he was selling rides for a dollar and a half. I desperately wanted to go. I wanted to go so badly, and my mother didn't have a dollar and a half. She said, "No, not this time, Madge. I can't do it now." I was so torn up about it that I grabbed hold of one of the wheels, and I hung onto it and cried. My mother untwisted me and took me home and told me just to be patient.

I guess aviation sort of became part of my subconscious. I was a student in college and I signed up for this civilian pilot training program and I was accepted, and my very first time in an airplane was my first flight lesson. The purpose of the whole program was to train pilots to be ready to fly when we got into the war, as we obviously were going to do. But in order to mask the military purpose of the program, they decided they would let one girl, to every ten boys, enroll.

After I finished the primary course and got my pilot's license, I went to sign up for the advanced course. They were only going to take ten students, but I was third in my class so I knew I qualified. I was told that the purpose of the course was to train men to fly in combat. So they were turning me down.

I went home, in my rage, and wrote Eleanor Roosevelt. I

Madge Minton standing in her living room with objects she has collected from around the world. Indianapolis, Indiana, 1995.

Madge Minton was twenty-two years old and engaged to be married when she joined the World War II Women Airforce Service Pilots (WASPs). Minton was assigned to fly fighter planes across the country to various military bases. Stationed in Long Beach, California, she was delivering pursuit planes including the P-40, P-39, P-47 Thunderbolt, and P-51 Mustangs after only two hours of ground instruction in each one. Minton appeared in *Life* magazine in July 1943 in an issue featuring the WASPs. She resigned from the WASPs in 1944 to start a family, and today she is an active member in the WASPs emeritus.

explained to her that I had been refused the advanced training which I had qualified for, because I was female. I felt wholly justified in writing the letter to the First Lady of the land, and I somehow knew in my heart that she would see it and that she would act on it, and she did. I suppose in all the things I've done in my life, that was probably the most significant, because it not only opened the door to the advanced training for me, it opened the door for the advanced training of women in the same program in colleges all over the country.

In January of 1943, I had a telegram asking me if I was interested in being a WASP, and that's the way it began. I was twenty-two years old, and had to report to Sweetwater, Texas, to the Avenger Air Field, for training.

When the first truckload of women were deposited at Avenger Field, the commander came out and said, "Who are you? I don't know anything about you. We have a flight training school here. We are well staffed and we have all the (in so many words) students we can handle. Just go away." And we went away. He called—this is not apocryphal—San Antonio, and he said, "What is this, anyway? What are these women doing in Avenger?" They told him that General Arnold had given him orders to accept us and to train us to fly military planes. We were in the Blue Bonnet Hotel in Sweetwater, and we all got back on the trucks. He accepted us and greeted us and cleaned out a couple of the barracks so that there would be room for us. The guys had to double up. We had, for about five or six weeks, a coeducational military flying

school, which would have been a scandal to the jaybirds. My mother would have come and taken me by the ear and taken me home if she'd known about it. I never told a soul until it was all over with.

Jackie [Cochran] came down to talk to us a couple of times. She would come in her own airplane, and she never wore a uniform while I was a cadet. There was nothing military about Jackie. She would come in a fancy hat and a fur coat, very chic and very pleasant. She believed in us and she backed us up. When we were going to be assigned to air bases over the country, each of us went to talk to her, individually, and she would ask what our preferences were. I mean, would we tow targets? Would we test-fly planes? Would we ferry bombers? I said that I wanted to be in the Air Transport Command ferrying division. I would like to ferry hot planes and big planes, and I wanted to be assigned to Long Beach, California, because my fiancé was stationed at the naval hospital in San Diego. She immediately gave her assent, and that's where I ended up, and I bless her for it. I had postponed my marriage. We were to be married on the seventeenth of April and I postponed it in order to become a pilot for the U.S. Air Force.

The BT-13A, which we called the Maytag Messerschmitt, was noisy, heavy, open. It had a sliding hatch. It was a powerful airplane, very maneuverable, had fixed landing gear. I didn't come across the retractable gear until I went in to advanced training, and that was the AT-6, the Texan, as it was called. It had a 600-horsepower engine and made a very satisfactory roar when you took off. As far as I expected to go was an AT-6. I loved the airplane. The first of the pursuit planes I flew was the P-40 Warhawk or Tomahawk. It was very interesting because it was so different from being trained to fly the other airplanes. In the pursuit planes, you got two hours of ground school for the airplane you were about to fly.

They took you out to the flight line, you got in the plane with your chute, you strapped yourself in, and the instructor was on the wing. He'd point out to you the mixture control and the throttle and the switch and all of the instruments which would be necessary to take off, fly, and land the airplane. After he had done that, he'd say, "Now, you show me." After he was satisfied that you knew them, he'd put a blindfold on you and he says, "Now, you're blindfolded, you can't see. Go through it again," and you'd do the same thing. You were very careful and very eager to learn because you want to fly that airplane.

After you did it successfully, blindfolded, he would climb down off the wing and say, "Be back in an hour," and walk away. And the airplane was yours and you'd never flown it, and that was a real thrill.

I have one very vivid recollection, just at the time when we were having a problem with the militarization of the WASPs. There were a lot of hard feelings and so on. I was ferrying a P-51, and I did an illegal thing. I took that P-51 off course and I pointed it northeast and I came to Indianapolis. I buzzed my hometown and I did outrageous things with that airplane. Sherman [husband] came to spend the night with me at my parents' house. The next day, we went out to the airport and I was so proud of that airplane, I walked him around the plane and I said, "This is my airplane and I have to take it to Newark." He said, "Very interesting," and walked away.

My husband had come back from overseas and I'd had a five-day pass to meet him in San Francisco. I went back and I ferried a couple of P-51s. I felt a little queasy, and I went to see the doctor and he said, "Did you ever think you might be pregnant?" At this time, the WASPs had already been voted against in Congress and they would be disbanded on the twenty-first of December. This was August. We were going to get kicked out anyway, and if I was carrying a child, I felt that I had a moral duty to protect the child. The doctor would have been obliged to report it to the authorities and I would have been kicked out, so to speak, and I preferred to resign.

I would have flown combat. I think this is the reason I've been so sympathetic to the contemporary women pilots about their problems. During that period of time, it was exactly the same point of justice I fought for in college. If they wanted to do it, let them do it. They earned it. I think women should have that privilege.

As a WASP emeritus, so to speak, I have been active going to meetings and so on. Then as many of us who could afford it, time and money, went to Washington for the hearings of the House of Representatives' Committee on Veteran Affairs and lobbied in person, and the bill was passed for our honorable discharges. I remember weeping like a fool out at the postbox when I got mine.

KIM DARST

Helicopter Pilot *Born February 27, 1969*

I was a very active kid, always running around outside. Nobody could ever find me. I thought I wanted to be a dolphin trainer or marine biologist somewhere like Sea World. I wanted to be one of the speakers, swim with the dolphins and get propelled off the dolphin's nose like you see with Shamu.

I guess the first time I went flying was when I was a junior in high school on a trip that my parents took me on. It was a helicopter scenic tour over the Grand Canyon. We called home, and my grandmother said, "Whatever you do, don't take a helicopter flight over the Grand Canyon because they just had a crash. Not a good idea." My father looked at me and said, "You know what that means?" I said, "Sure, we've got to go." Because we defy orders all the time.

We took the ride, and I got to sit in the front because I was the lightest of the passengers. We were in a Jet Ranger and I don't remember the Grand Canyon. I was watching all the instruments and trying to figure everything out. It was only about a twenty-minute flight and I decided that's what I wanted to do.

My parents drove me up to Ellensville, New York, for flight instruction because I didn't have my driver's license yet. It was a two-hour drive one way. Hovering is the hardest thing that you can do in a helicopter, and that's basically standing still about three feet off the ground. My instructor told me, "You gotta start working your feet 'cause your feet keep the nose straight in the helicopter. Do you dance?" I said, "No." He said, "I really suggest that you take dancing lessons, ballet lessons or something like that." I actually came out crying to my mom. I said, "I am not going to take dancing lessons. I really want to learn how to fly a helicopter but if it means taking dancing lessons, I'm not so sure." I never took them.

I wanted to do something different [for high school graduation].

....

Kim Darst in her office. Blairstown, New Jersey, 1993.

Kim Darst purchased her first helicopter when she was nineteen years old and is now the owner of K.D. Helicopters. She teaches flight and ground instruction in a Bell-47-G2 helicopter and Cessna airplanes with a clientele of eleven helicopter students and forty airplane students. Darst is a licensed airframe and powerplant mechanic and performs most of the maintenance on her helicopter and two airplanes. At twenty-two years old she became the youngest Federal Aviation Administration (FAA) helicopter flight examiner in the country and holds an FAA Inspector Authorization rating. She resides with her parents in Blairstown, New Jersey.

Everyone drives in cars or limousines, or something like that so I decided I would fly in. I had a friend who had a Jet Ranger, let's say a $350,000 helicopter, and he said, "Go right to it." We [flight instructor] both flew into the graduation and I hopped out of the helicopter—I flew in sneakers—and put on my dress shoes and walked over and got my diploma, sat through graduation, and hopped back in the helicopter and took off.

A week after graduation I moved to New York and lived alone in a motor home and worked at an airport. I worked as an apprentice airframe and powerplant mechanic, doing everything and anything. I was tearing apart engines, putting fabric on an airplane, and then I would wash and wax things, pump gas, and do paperwork. I got my flight instruction rating and did all of the flight instruction.

I found a helicopter that October and the guy wanted $55,000. I wanted the helicopter but said, "No, I can't afford it." So about December I called again and it was still there. I asked some more questions about it, and said I couldn't afford it. February came around and I came to my father and said, "You know, I really want that helicopter." He said, "Go buy it." And I said, "Oh, yeah?" He said, "I'll back the loan for you, but the first time you don't make a payment on the loan, you sell the machine!" I was nineteen at the time.

My mom said, "If you are going to buy it, you've got to have a corporation, and you have to start your own business." So that's basically how I got started in the business because I needed a way to pay off the heli-copter and I couldn't do it with the salary of a normal job. I have never really flown that helicopter for fun. I don't think I've ever taken a trip with it. It's always been strictly business. So I started with just a helicopter and three students.

Since I am an airframe and powerplant mechanic, I have a habit of getting everything greasy so all my good clothes are in a different closet so I don't wear them, especially my white shirts. My mom, she sees me wear anything good, she says, "Nope" and hides my clothes. Every once in a while I'll do speeches for career day at the schools and I'll say, "Where's that shirt? Where are my good clothes?" And she'll have them hidden so I don't get them all greasy.

My parents are great in moral support. We're a very close family personal-wise and also business-wise. But as far as money is concerned, they don't have a dime in the helicopter or the airplanes. My father did back the loan on the helicopter and then after I started paying off the helicopter I had enough collateral basically to buy my own two airplanes, to get the loans without him backing them. I had a lot of students who assumed my father bought the machines, and he did *not*.

Right now I have a real good reputation and I do not advertise at all. Everyone comes here by word of mouth. Most people think it's great that I own the business, and that I took the initiative to start it, go into debt as much as I did, and buy these things and try to work them off. I run around here like a nut seven days a week. I've worked every holiday that there is. I've actually soloed some people on Christmas Day.

Kim Darst with her mother, Darla Darst, at K.D. Helicopters. Blairstown, New Jersey, 1993.

PATTY WAGSTAFF

Aerobatic Pilot *Born September 11, 1951*

Patty Wagstaff with the German monoplane Extra 260. Andrews Air Force Base, Maryland, 1993.

When you first start doing it, you feel like your head's going to explode and your eyeballs are going to pop out. All the blood drains out of your head and goes down to your feet so you have to tense your stomach muscles and your chest muscles, and then if it really gets bad, you tense up in your neck. I'm pulling so many Gs in such a short amount of time, it's automatic with me. Going from positive to negative so quickly is what really gives you an amazing physical sensation. There is so much going on and so many things you have to look at with the airplane, the temperatures and pressures of the engine, the air speed, and where you are in the box, you really don't have time to think about it.

When I first started competing, none of the women in aerobatics had any visions of being national champion. It was just being victims of that kind of thinking, just the way I probably was as a kid when my parents told me I couldn't be an airline pilot. I just accepted it. Women are under so much more scrutiny than men, in aviation. I mean, if you make a mistake, you get more crap over it. If you don't fly as well, you don't ever get as far as the men. There's a lot of men that aren't brilliant pilots and they do fine in aviation careers, but women have to be better.

I really had to teach myself to want to win. I had to force myself to dig deep for that anger that you have when you are in high school—when you are just angry at the world and just ready to go out and kick some butt or drive your car too fast, however it manifests itself. I had to really look for that because I was too laid back. I said, "I don't care about winning. I just want to fly, and I'm so lucky to be able to do this." But it started to come to me and now I'm very competitive.

Competition is a mental game in any sport. I start preparing mentally months before. When I get in bed at night, I go through a

Patty Wagstaff became the first woman to win the National Aerobatic Championship in 1991, since the men's and women's competitions were merged in 1972. She defended the title in 1992 and 1993. Her yearly schedule alternates between major regional, national, and international competitions and air shows. She is a six-time member of the U.S. aerobatic team, which competes in world competition every two years. Her home base is in Tucson, Arizona, where she practices and gives instruction in aerobatics. She has also flown as an exhibition pilot for major motion pictures.

routine every night for months, sometimes for three months. I'll go through the routines in my mind and it sort of lulls me to sleep. And I fly it. Sometimes I'm outside the plane. Sometimes I'm inside. And it's always from a little different angle, and the wind is always different. If you have that kind of focus and know that you have to train mentally to do all the right things, you can't help but succeed. It's just preparation. If I get really nervous, I take my hand and just bang myself on the leg.

For years I'd go to the nationals or the other contests and a starter at the aerobatic contest would come up to me and make sure all my belts were strapped in and release me into the box, and he'd always go, "Now, you kick ass." He's a big old gruff guy. "You kick ass. I want to see you win." He would always give me this lecture. So one day he came up with this little [kick ass] sticker and put it in the cockpit. Now every plane I get, they always have it in there when I pick up the plane.

[In high school] I was the class clown and I was always in trouble—not in a real evil way. I went to some very strict Catholic-type girls' schools. Big mistake for me. I just wanted to be around the guys. They had all the fun. I raised mice in my desk and sold the babies. I sowed my oats the way boys were supposed to. I used to say, "If I was a boy, it would be expected of me to do these kinds of things." But girls weren't expected to do that. I was always in trouble and getting kicked out of schools.

In 1970 I was kind of a hippie and I hitchhiked across the country. I traveled a lot, had a backpack, went hiking, and had friends that lived in sort of a commune up in Northern California. It was a really exciting time to be around—I was in Japan for part of it, and in San Francisco a little bit. I did a lot of different things. I lived in England for a while and I was a chauffeur, I did modeling jobs, although I never really enjoyed that very much. I did office work, waitressing, things like that. I wanted to experience everything. I dreamed about being a spy, because you could fly and you could climb mountains—fantasy stuff.

In 1983 Bob [Wagstaff] took me to an air show and to an aerobatic competition. I had already started flying, and I was working on my instructor's rating but had never taken aerobatic lessons. I'll never forget how frustrated I was just sitting there watching the air show going on and all the pilots interacting with each other and the planes behind the fence. It was very difficult for me to be a spectator. I really wanted to get out there and do it. I just knew it was something I could do and something I could do well.

Lucking into aviation the way I did, running into it, or being able to do it at the time I did, it was like I was looking for something. I wasn't out there sort of desperate, but in the back of my mind I knew there was something that I was going to find my little niche in. It was just a matter of time, and aviation was it. As soon as I started flying, I knew this is where I needed to be. I really needed a challenge and a focus and I wanted to achieve something. I wanted to make my mark somewhere. Aviation just symbolized everything that I loved. It was freedom, total freedom. You can get in an airplane, you can leave, you can go somewhere else, and you can be up there all by yourself. You grab hold of the stick in the plane and everything is sort of right. The world's at peace.

It's perfect being on the air circuit. I know how to live on the road. I love getting rid of my stuff and having a bare minimum of things. It makes me feel really free. I hate being tied down to the house and having all this stuff. I hate collecting things. I love to give things away. The air show circuit's wonderful, and the longer I'm on the road in the summer, the more I get into it and the more I enjoy it. I usually start traveling in mid-May or so, and then I'm gone pretty much until the end of October.

Whatever your religious beliefs are, there's something very powerful and spiritual about aviation. Anybody that flies has felt that feeling that somebody's out there looking out for them. You really need to listen to your instincts in flying. It's really important. Anytime you go against your better judgment in aviation, probably in anything, it's a mistake.

In the early days I've had the plane get into a flat spin and I had trouble getting out of it. Generally, you don't have time to be afraid. If something goes wrong, you react to it and then you're afraid afterwards. You immediately take care of the situation, look around, hope you do the right thing, hope

Patty Wagstaff visualizing her flying routine before an aerobatic competition. Warrenton, Virginia, 1995.

Patty Wagstaff sitting on the hand-built German monoplane Extra 260, the airplane in which she won the National Aerobatic Championship in 1991 and 1992. Andrews Air Force Base, Maryland, 1993.

you've practiced your emergency procedures, and you are not thinking in terms of fear or nerves or butterflies or anything like that. And really, afterwards there's no reason to be afraid if you've taken care of the situation. You really just don't have time for it. I've never been afraid flying up in the air. No need to be.

I've seen accidents and I've lost some good friends. But it happens and you learn to deal with it and you learn to live with it. I've gone through all sorts of stages with it— losing friends, like being mildly depressed for a year, or wondering if I should continue. I did think maybe it's inevitable. I think you tend to develop a little bit of a fatalistic attitude when that happens to you. It's just a by-product of it. But I worked through it. My attitude now is that life's short and I'm here, I'm alive, and, you know, we're all going to be gone pretty soon.

I've really accomplished what I wanted to do with winning the nationals. I wanted to win three times. But what I really want to do is to go to the nationals and fly my best. That's really hard to do when you feel like you have to win. Last year I flew the nationals, I did well. I won by a good margin, but I never flew my best. I was nervous and I was so tense, because I wanted to win. I just knew I had to do it. So it really affected my flying. It was dreadful. I can fly much better than this—I know I can. You have very few flights that are your best when you are actually in the competition. Most of them are in practice.

AEROBATIC TEAM
ENGLAND ★
CANADA
SWITZERLAND
1992 FRANCE
States National
batic Champion
1991
1992 ★

USA
AEROBATIC TEAM

IDA VAN SMITH-DUNN

Pilot *Born March 21, 1917*

As I grew up, there was no one in North Carolina or nearby states that we could find who would teach me to fly, even when I was in high school. I wanted to fly, and my father was looking around and trying to find somebody. They said that they didn't have any instructors. But the planes were there. Now, I don't know if they didn't have any instructors or not, but I think maybe they did. I knew then that even if they had instructors, that they weren't going to teach any black people to fly. I didn't cry about it because I was really involved with my studies in high school. I knew that somewhere along the line, if I continued to be interested, I would learn to fly.

While I was studying at New York University working on my doctorate degree, one day without saying a word, I got up, went outside to my car, drove to La Guardia Airport, and had my first flight lesson. Nobody at my house knew where I was, nobody in the world knew where I was, none of my acquaintances. So the flight instructor and I flew over the Hudson River, around, and he showed me different maneuvers and everything. I was just—talking about *in* air, then I was *on* air. I was so delighted because I had been wanting to do that for so long.

"Girl, you know you're going to break your neck up there!" Oh, everybody tried to discourage me, because I wasn't a youngster when I started. I was fifty, a very, very exciting fifty. But it came easy. It was because I was so enthusiastic about it, I guess. But I had some darn good instructors.

The first time my instructor sent me to do a solo flight, he sent me to Lumberton, North Carolina. There was a guy that used to work for my father who saw me bring the plane in. I had to go in and get my book signed, then I came back out and took off. He came to the barbershop that night and said, "Oh, I saw that little Larkin girl flying an

Ida Van Smith-Dunn reflects on her childhood dream to fly. Lumberton, North Carolina, 1994.

Ida Van Smith-Dunn founded the Ida Van Smith Flight Clubs, Inc. in 1967. The flight club teaches children about aviation through a ground school course on the history of the aviation industry and the basic mechanics of navigation and operating the aircraft. Talks from experts in the air industry and arranged field trips to airports for free flights and to air industry–related facilities supplement the course. Accumulating many awards for her promotion of aviation education, she was honored in 1978 by the World Aerospace Educators.

airplane right by herself today"—my maiden name was Larkin. So the others said, "Oh, stop lying. You know you didn't see any little Larkin girl flying that plane." "Yes, I did." Well, they kept it up, so that a fight broke out. They had to call the police, and some of them were hauled off to jail. That was just terrible, because they didn't believe it.

On my second solo flight my flight instructor sent me back to Lumberton again, so my family met me there. Three southern gentlemen came into [the airport] and my family heard them say, "Well God almighty, did you see what I saw?" The other one said, "Blankety-blank (cursing), yes, I saw it. By God!" And the other one said, "What is the world coming to? They got *them* flying now." But we never knew if they meant they got the blacks flying them now or if they got the women flying them now.

The kids heard there was a black woman out at Fayetteville Airport, in North Carolina, and they would come to watch. When I would land the plane and start to my car where it was parked, they would waylay me. I was in no mood, because I wanted to get home and hit those books as fast as I could, but I always stopped and talked to them, and they would ask me so many questions. Some of them I didn't even know the answer yet. And I said to them, "I'll look it up and tell you tomorrow," which I did. You know, you really have to be honest with kids, especially with something like that. I spent a lot of time with them. Every day it happened. So that's how the flight clubs started.

When the announcement came out that I was going to teach the Aviation Career

Ida Van Smith-Dunn with children from her flight club at the Lumberton County Airport. Lumberton, North Carolina, 1994.

Exposure Program at York College in New York, two hundred people applied. I planned to take, say, thirty people, but I extended it to forty. It was rather interesting for passersby to come and see this woman teaching aviation to this class. It just happened that the room they assigned to me was right on the front by the sidewalk and with large glass windows, so that people would come and watch. I was surprised that some of them would stay there for an hour just staring.

There was nothing about managing a plane and flying a plane that was too difficult, too heavy, in any way that they [the students] couldn't handle. It's not like having to lift a hundred-pound weight or something. All they needed was the brainpower. There were some from affluent families, but some of the kids I had in the classes came from very, very poor, poor homes in Queens, and they had almost nothing. But I talked with the parents and encouraged them to make certain that the kids didn't stay out of school for any reason whatsoever. It just turned out to be very nice, because mention aviation and one kid would say, "I've taken aviation." The next kid, he wants it. Another kid will want it, see, and it just goes around. To them, it seemed to have meant prestige, you see, because it was so new to them. It was new to me, too. To tell you the truth, it was new to me.

When I met the kids I always said to them, we're not trying to make pilots out of everyone, but we want you to know that you can be a pilot if you want to be, or whatever else you want to pursue in life, you can do it.

SUSAN PIERCE

Hang Glider Pilot *Born June 7, 1963*

You're out in the open and you're part of the elements. You feel like it's you flying, not the plane flying. You don't have the protection of an aircraft. This is just me. I thank God for the view when I'm up there, for the beautiful world that He's created. A lot of times I also pray that He will help me get down safely when I'm getting tossed around by turbulence and I'm afraid.

Birds are master pilots, so we will often watch to see what kind of altitude they're getting, how tight their turns are. If we're ready to launch, and we see several birds circling right out in front of us and going up, we'll dive out into that same area and go up with them. In essence, they've marked a thermal for us. I've been wingtip to wingtip with birds before. They'll dive out of the trees into the air with you. We're moving at about the same speed as the birds.

Some of our launches are flat, sloping grassy areas with trees off to the sides, and some of our sites are slots cut into the top of a mountain with trees close in on the sides and down below. That's very intimidating, because sometimes you cannot tell ahead of time whether you're really going to clear the trees. You just have to trust that other people have flown the site and they've missed the treetops down below and you probably will, too. Our favorite site is a cliff launch, and it's got a shear cliff, I would say probably sixty feet high, with trees down below that.

[To safely launch in strong winds] you have a wire crew consisting of three to five people hanging on to the wires on the sides of your glider and on to your keel. They keep you from pitching over the edge until your wings are stable, the wind is coming in steady, and you yell, "Clear." They let go and you push off the edge of the cliff.

In order to fly well, you need to understand pitch, yaw, and roll controls, just like any other pilot, but the way you control these

Susan Pierce with her Moyes XtraLite 137 hang glider. McConnellsburg, Pennsylvania, 1994.

Susan Pierce took up hang gliding as an adult, a goal she set as a child after seeing a hang glider in the movie *To Fly* at the National Air and Space Museum. Flying since 1991, she is at the intermediate level (Hang III) and competes on the national level. Working as an architect and vice president of Home Remodelers Inc., a business based from her home, she has the luxury to step out of the office and go flying when the weather is favorable. Unlike most aircraft, her Moyes XtraLite 137 glider can be transported on the top of her truck to wherever she chooses to lift off from and is assembled before each flight.

Susan Pierce preparing to
launch her hang glider.
McConnellsburg,
Pennsylvania, 1994.

three things are with shifts in body weight, which is very unlike other types of aviation. You have no control surfaces. It's not a matter of pulling a lever; it's a matter of using your arm muscles to shift your body weight. If you want to go right, you shift your body to the right. Left, shift to the left. Speed up, you pull the bar in toward you. Slow down, you push the bar out. You have to be careful not to stall or go into a slipping turn too close to the ground. There are a lot of nuances. It's a lot of finesse, I would say.

I have to exercise in order to stay in shape to fly. I lift weights and ride an exercise bicycle. I have to keep my cardio-vascular system healthy, and I have to stay flexible and strong, because the inputs you give to the glider are purely physical. And the glider weighs seventy-five pounds, and if I didn't stay in shape, I wouldn't be able to even carry my own glider.

You are allowed to land anywhere you want. But most of the fields we land in are cow pastures or alfalfa fields or cornfields, and we designate a field. For each launch site that we have, there's a designated landing field that you usually land in unless you decide to fly down the ridge or over the back of the mountain and try to get some miles. Then you just pick a field that looks good and hope the landowner is friendly— and that he isn't keeping a bull in the field.

Once you land, [getting back to the launch site] entirely depends on the situation. If there's a nice farmer that just insists that he's going to drive you back, or if there's someone you can bribe with a twenty-dollar bill, it might take only a few minutes. I once hitchhiked a ride to a sheriff's office and then got a ride by that sheriff to the border of his county, then another sheriff from the next county picked me up and took me to my car. That took a long time.

On one flight I came in on my final approach to land, and I just kept going and going and going. The field was falling away from me. This field was huge, and my feelings went from "Oh, yeah, this is great," to "Wow, oh, man, I don't think I'm going to come down." Finally at the end: "I'm going to hit those trees!" So I flared just as I got to the trees, and I came up very gently against the trees. I reached out and grabbed a branch, and I just thought, "Whew. I'm okay." Just at that second, the branch broke, and I tumbled backwards out of the tree. The glider hit the ground. I landed on my head on top of the glider and hurt my neck, but if I hadn't landed on top of the glider, I might have been in a lot worse shape than that.

You get an adrenaline rush from doing this. It makes me feel like I'm strong and I can accomplish something. I'd always wanted to do it, so this is a fulfillment of something I decided when I was about ten or twelve years old. Oh, you feel so good when you land after a good flight. You compare notes with your buddies. You analyze your flight and you drive home just glowing.

SUSAN STILL

Lieutenant, United States Navy, Combat Pilot and Astronaut *Born October 24, 1961*

I wanted to be a hairdresser when I grew up. I'd sit on the back of the sofa and my mother would sit in front of me, and as long as it didn't involve scissors or dye, she'd let me do whatever I wanted to her hair. All the women in my life were nurses, hairdressers, or secretaries, and that's why I thought my father would not support me in being a pilot. I can remember asking him, "What would you think if I told you I wanted to be a pilot when I grow up?" expecting him to say no or disagree. He said, "I think that would be fantastic." Had he not said those words, I don't know what would have happened to me.

I went to a private boarding school up in Massachusetts for high school, and as part of the senior year, they let seniors write a proposal as to what they could do in one month's time that would be career-enhancing. I had proposed to get my private pilot's license in that time. I needed the forty hours to take my flying test and I flew every single day unless the weather was too bad. My first solo, I was pretty scared. I was young and only had four hours of instruction. I found out later that there was a bet between my instructor and another guy's instructor that he could solo me before the other guy soloed his student.

I had no concept of the military or military airplanes at all. Never in a million years would it have occurred to me to join the military until Dick Scobee [*Challenger* commander] suggested it. When I worked for Lockheed after college, my boss hooked me up with him because I was interested in the space program and wanted to know what would be the best way of getting into it. So I talked with him on the phone a couple of times and his recommendation was that I join the military as a pilot. So that was exactly why I joined the military to become a pilot, because Dick Scobee told me to.

My oldest brother told me that he didn't think women should be

Lieutenant Susan Still, USN, in her flight suit at the Patuxent River Naval Air Station, Maryland, 1993.

Susan Still, Lieutenant, USN, was the third woman selected by the U.S. Navy to be trained in combat aircraft for attack missions. Entering the Navy in 1986 to become a test pilot, she transitioned to the Grumman F-14 Tomcat when military combat training was made available to women in 1993. Previously, she had worked at Lockheed as an aeronautical engineer while earning an M.S. in aerospace engineering at the Georgia Institute of Technology. She came closer to her long-term goal of becoming an astronaut in 1994 when she was selected by NASA as an astronaut (pilot). Her first space flight is scheduled for spring 1997.

in combat. He appreciated that it was my decision, but he didn't think women should be in combat. I can't say that all the guys agree, but typically what I have found is that most of the men agree that women can do the job as far as being a pilot. I'd say most of the men don't want women in the ready rooms or on the ship with them for a variety of reasons—camaraderie, they think, will be sacrificed, or their families, their wives, will be upset or whatever the case may be. But I found that individually, I've been accepted after I've proved myself. So they're willing to accept me but they're not willing to say, across the board, yes, let's integrate women and go for it.

A lot of places [locker rooms] will try to section off an area just for the women or put curtains up so the men can go back there or whatever. We all wear long underwear and I don't have any problem with people seeing me in long underwear. I mean, it's men's long underwear that they issue you, anyway. As far as the men, I've seen them in various stages of dress and undress. I've never had a problem with it.

The F-14 community has a reputation of being the most macho, chauvinistic community in the Navy, and from my own personal experience, I tend to agree with that. How would I be treated? I was in ground school for four months before I flew my first flight [in a Grumman F-14 Tomcat], so my anxiety had built up by the time I flew. Some of the guys didn't really quite understand, but I knew at the end of my first flight, before I got my flight gear off and got upstairs, everybody in the building would know how I

did on my flight as the first woman to fly in that squadron. It would have been different had I gotten here and flown the next week, but I had been here for months listening to people's ideas about women and stuff. So there was a lot of pressure on me.

That first flight was one of the hardest flights in my life, because the airplane had a lot of problems. We ended up having to shut down an engine and couldn't get it restarted. We had a hydraulic problem on top of that, and so we had to use some backup systems to get the landing gear down and the flaps down. There wasn't a good horizon and I had lost my primary attitude information. So there were all these problems, and I ended up having to take an arrested landing at the field. In retrospect, it was the best thing that could have happened, because the whole flight was just a disaster and I handled it as I had been trained in the simulator and it all worked out fine. There was no more pressure after that.

Some of the most dynamic flying that I did in the Tomcat was shooting the banner. I mean, everything happens in a split second. You're pulling a lot of Gs, your arms are getting tired, you're having to get your airplane in the exact piece of sky it needs to be in, at the speed and altitude it needs to be at, and you're using your radar to get the pipper on the bull's eye on the banner and making sure all your switches are right to shoot the bullets, and you've got two other airplanes out there that you have to keep in sight at the same time. So it's like you need about six more eyeballs and two more hands and another foot to do it all, but it's very fun when it all comes together and everybody's doing what they're supposed to do. You're going fast and it's loud and you're pulling a lot of Gs and you get done with the flight and you're just sweating.

When I was in Key West, the bad guys were another squadron and I think it was the first time they had flown against a woman ever, I think that was kind of an interesting situation. I mean, nobody likes to get shot at, but I think it was even worse when they heard it from a woman, "Fox two," meaning that the missiles are coming at them, or "Guns, guns, guns," meaning bullets are coming at them.

There was a lot of talk going around about Kara Hultgreen [the first woman F-14 pilot, who crashed while attempting a carrier landing] and her qualifications. I'd flown with her, and she was an excellent pilot. The media made a big deal about her disqualling at the boat. Well, over one-third of all F-14 student pilots disqual the first time; over one-third, I mean, it's like 38 percent or something. So the fact that she disqualled is not a surprise. First of all, the time period since she had carrier-qualled before was a lot greater than any other student because she had been flying in non-combat positions for three years, so she was not getting a look at the boat again as soon as everybody else was. So that could have led to her problems. It's hard to say.

I had requested not to do any PR [public relations] stuff while I was in training, because I wanted the exact same consideration as the guys had, and the guys weren't doing any PR stuff. It's not so much

that interviews take time, because that's a small part of it, but it's that it sets you apart from the men and you're no longer one of the guys. Getting through this program is a group effort. It's a team. You help each other and you share information. It's way too much information for any one person to gather, so you share information and you discuss techniques and things you learned in your flight. If I'm off doing interviews and having cameramen following me around, then I'm no longer part of the team. Now I'm like the prima donna, regardless of whether I asked to do it or not. The guys see it as getting special treatment, so during training, I asked not to do that. After I'm done with training, then, by all means, let the press at me because it's new for women to be doing this and I'll do my part to support it. I feel like I've been given a gift and that I ought to pay it back, when I can.

I was slated to go out to the USS *Eisenhower* as the token woman F-14 pilot when they got set to sail, but before I was finished with my training here, I got accepted with the astronaut program, so I didn't ever go to sea. I think that when we have our next air battle, I'll be a little sad that I'm not there with my friends, doing my part, because I've been trained so much for it. But on the other hand, the whole reason I joined the Navy was to be an astronaut. I wanted to do that from the beginning, so it's a fair tradeoff.

MARY ELLEN WEBER

Astronaut *Born August 24, 1962*

I was seven years old when they walked on the moon, and I remember it very clearly. We watched it at my grandmother's house in Garfield Heights, Ohio. We were in the living room and we were staying up. I remember my mom. When [the astronauts] were there on the moon, she said, "Okay, you're there. Now get back. Get back in and come home." It was a very tense, exciting time. I remember the *Apollo 13* mishap, and the prospect that these astronauts might not make it back home.

People ask me about the risk and fear a lot. It's really interesting, because every day people get on two-lane highways and it would take the slightest turn of the wheel by the [oncoming driver] to get into a head-on collision that would kill you, and yet nobody thinks about that. We wear seat belts and do what we can to make it safe, but we say that having the transportation mobility is worth that risk. That's the same approach I think the astronauts take.

The bulk of the training that all astronauts do focuses on how to fly and operate the shuttle. The shuttle is an *extremely* complex beast, and we need to understand how every system works—the environmental system, the hydraulic system, the electrical system—and how they interact. The main engines, the guidance and navigation, everything you can imagine we need to learn. You're working as a crew, and it is incredibly challenging to master the shuttle and to integrate all of these different systems.

Water training and EVA [extravehicular activity] training is very difficult. It continues to surprise me how difficult the task is; it's one of the most physically demanding things that we do. One of the veteran astronauts described it as trying to knit with boxing gloves. Whenever you see people actually doing space walks, they make it look so easy and so graceful, but you're really working against this

Mary Ellen Weber during survival training before her space flight. Water Environmental Training Facility (WETF), NASA. Johnson Space Center, Houston, Texas, 1995.

Mary Ellen Weber, Ph.D., served as mission specialist onboard the space shuttle *Discovery* flight STS-70 in June of 1995. Her duties included middeck experiments such as using the bioreactor with the intention to grow human tissues in microgravity space, and she was one of two crew members to deploy the TDRS (Tracking and Data Relay Satellite). She also spoke with high school students on ham radio contacts from space. She became interested in aviation after taking a skydiving lesson in college. She is an instrument rated pilot and received silver medals in the U.S. national skydiving competition in 1991 and 1995.

Mary Ellen Weber suspended over a swimming pool during survival training. WETF, NASA. Johnson Space Center, Houston, Texas, 1995.

pressure suit. Every movement you do is hindered by it. But it's a lot of fun. You feel like the Michelin man. You are inflated. You're wearing this balloon. You have so many other things pushing and pulling and constricting, you don't even know you're wearing a diaper, if that gives you some indication of how bulky that thing is. Eventually you find out if you have something digging into you and they'll put a pad there, and eventually it feels like it's yours. That's been happening slowly with each successive run that I make.

We spent a lot of time doing survival training, which we need for bailout scenarios. They taught us how to make shelters out of parachutes, how to fend for ourselves, how to catch rabbits, how to set up snares. In water survival, both with the T-38s and with our shuttle system, we have rafts, and you have to learn how to use those and how to get yourself out of the exposure, get in the raft, cover yourself up, and keep warm. Even warm water can be very cold. In the Atlantic (which is where we would bail out if you had a shuttle scenario), they project we could stay alive for about twenty hours before we would die of thermal exposure. So it's really important that you do things correctly so that you don't die before that time.

Mission specialists fly in the back seat of the T-38, and the astronaut pilots fly in the front seat. There are a lot of reasons why we fly the T-38s. We do things with simulators, but if you want to train for reacting and responding to real-time, high-speed, dynamic environment, you need the real thing as part of the training. You're moni-

toring systems, you're working with other crew members, speaking over the radios, which sounds like a trivial thing, except everything we do gets transmitted to the world. The other thing is that when we do ascents and entries, we wear suits and parachutes and helmets and you're in this confining environment in which you're working and flying and pulling out checklists and referring to things, and we get to actually do that in the T-38.

[On my mother's perspective:] My father died when I was a baby, so it was just my mom. For her, doing these things probably wouldn't outweigh the risk. I don't think she would ever actually want to go up in a rocket. She had known I had been skydiving for many years and had basically [resigned] herself to the fact that I was going to do these things that she considered dangerous. She knew how much it meant to me, and no matter whether she was afraid or not, she was very supportive.

[On role models:] People covet what they see. You want to be what you see around you when you're a little kid. I didn't know any pilots. I knew engineers. I liked science, but I saw engineers. Nobody directly around me, certainly no women, were doctors or lawyers. It's not that I didn't know they existed, but it wasn't what I saw around me. And so I never considered being a pilot. I think if I hadn't been so far away from home and got exposed to new things and new people, I don't think I ever would have done something like skydiving. It was sort of through skydiving that I got into flying.

[On role models from Purdue University:]

Amelia Earhart is bigger than life. She was so far removed, she didn't seem real. Even though Amelia taught [at Purdue University] and she did these great things, you don't necessarily associate that with yourself. There are a lot of astronauts that have gone to Purdue, and Purdue makes that known to their students. I think that was where I first was introduced to the fact that these people did not seem bigger than life to me. These people seemed like engineers that went to Purdue.

When I finally did apply [to the astronaut program], I was thrilled to get an interview, because I really thought that's as far as I would go. I thought it would be a chance in a lifetime to see NASA for a week and actually get to see things close up. I couldn't imagine that it would actually work out that they would pick me over all these other people. A lot of people ask me, "What does it take to be an astronaut?" You have to have the right credentials, you have to be qualified, but I think the overwhelming thing is luck.

As far as what I hope to accomplish, it's something that's real prevalent in the astronaut office. You can't have a bunch of people who are interested in achieving their own individual goals. You're a team, and I know it sounds like a cliché, but [for] mission success, you do what it takes, if that means cleaning out the toilet or whatever. There are so many roles to play as mission specialist and I would like to play them all. Being an effective crew member and making the mission successful, that's what I'm striving for.

118

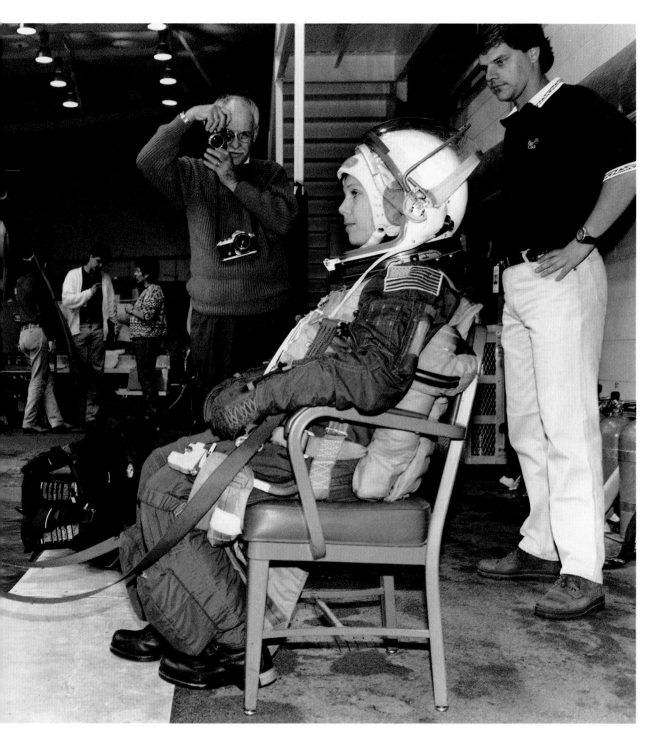

Mary Ellen Weber being photographed by Andrew Patnesky, NASA's staff photographer. WETF, NASA. Johnson Space Center, Houston, Texas, 1995.

GAYLE RANNEY

Alaskan Bush Pilot *Born May 22, 1940*

I just don't know how people live without getting out to see what's going on. If I'm on the ground one day, I start to get restless, because I want to see. I want to see where the animals are and I want to see what the seasonal changes are and how the fishermen are doing with their nets and check out the surf. There are wonderful vantage points.

The bush is anything that's out beyond populated areas. In Alaska, a populated area might be two hundred or three hundred people, and the bush is beyond that. All of this country is not serviced by anything but small airplanes. We do whatever people need to have done. We have a mail contract out of Cordova, and people receive their mail and they can also ride on the mail planes. We carry the commercial fishermen and their gear, and their pets, kids, anything that they need. We also do fish hauling. [From] some of the rivers you can't get to the processing plant, like the Dry Bay processing plant; the only way you can get the fish in is by small airplane. So we fill our airplane with totes and containers and bring the fish in.

My son and I have specialized in animal research projects, so we do quite a bit of telemetry work, which is where the animals are collared, and we track them with antennas on the airplanes. Then it's just a matter of listening to the receiver and finding the animals. We do a lot of animal counts, too, the actual counting of the critters. We've worked with sea otters in Prince William Sound, and mountain goats. The moose are fun to watch, and certainly the most fun when they're having their calves in the spring. Wolves are some of the most fascinating, wonderful animals in the world. The wolf population in this area is much less than in other areas, and the feeding that the wolves do is different, too. But without this information, how do we know? We have nothing to base the man-

Gayle Ranney taking a rare break at her Yakutat base of Fishing and Flying, Yakutat, Alaska, 1993.

Gayle Ranney is a bush pilot in southeast Alaska. After working for various air-taxi operations over a span of nineteen years, she and her son founded their own business, Fishing and Flying, in 1985. Based in Cordova, the business offers private charters, fishing trips, sightseeing tours, and delivers the U.S. mail. The business also specializes in providing service to animal researchers for animal telemetry work and to the United States Geological Survey for researchers studying the Bering Glacier. Flying airplanes equipped with floats, skis, and wheels, the company is outfitted with seven aircraft, four pilots, and four mechanics.

agement on. We do share a strong sense of responsibility to the animals, and it gives us a chance to actually have an effect.

We're watching some *major* changes in Alaska now, changes that we never dreamed we would see. A lot of development is happening because it's finally economically feasible to come up and take the resources. So we're seeing an encroachment on the wilderness. As long as we have people and animals in the same area, then things aren't in just a natural order. I'm not what you would call an extreme environmentalist, but I'm one who wants to see part of Alaska retained.

I never went to flight schools, and everything I did was the hard route. I took a little Taylorcraft and [almost] wore out the Juneau runway because that's where I learned to fly. I spent a lot of time listening to people and I learned to sort out the bullshit from the real stuff very quickly. I would just listen and go out and test things out. I went into some fairly interesting places, some of them I never went back to for obvious reasons, and it was like, "Oh, Lord, if you let me get out of here, I'll promise I'll never come back in again." But, oh, my goodness, what an exciting part of the learning process! I mean, the adrenaline would really flow.

Once I was flying an airplane [alone] that the artificial horizon had gone out on and I got into whiteout conditions, in a white ball of nothing. I was in zero-zero visibility, I could see the wingtips and that was all. I had the skis down because I knew I was in deep doo-doo. When I touched down, you know, it just felt like a real light landing. I thought,

Gayle Ranney taking a walk outside her cabin on the Doame River. Yakutat, Alaska, 1993.

123

"Wow, I got away with it." But unbeknownst to me, one of the gear got knocked off. So that meant that when it settled down the second time that I also got the prop. So I was there. A couple of days. Sat it out.

No way you could leave the airplane. It was ninety-mile-an-hour winds, and the wind chill factor was probably thirty below. It was an absolutely desolate place, so there's nothing you could do but just sit it out in the plane, which is a very cold thing. I had a couple of prunes. I've hated prunes ever since. The wind was blowing so hard that I just hoped that it didn't just tumble the plane. I thought about wiring the doors shut, because after you lose so much sleep, and as hypothermia sets in, you know, your mind will start playing tricks on you too. You could not go outside. There were no choices. You really had to keep your mind disciplined. In that situation you couldn't think about anything but just taking care of yourself and surviving the best you could.

What you're carrying in your pockets is your survival kit. What you have in your survival box, that's your luxury kit. And that's the way to look at it, because if something did happen, you might not get back to the airplane.

When I started my career it was really tough, especially since the boys were eight and ten and I was a single parent. My sons and I had a routine we worked out, and right before I'd come home at the end of the day, I'd circle the house and that was sort of, "Clean up the house and get ready. Here comes Mom."

I worked long, hard hours and there was no give in the business. Either I did the job, or somebody else was going to take the job. I took four years off from commercial flying to go fishing out of Yakutat. I just needed a break from it, not from the flying but from the other side of it. You are by yourself in this, and you really don't have an opportunity to sit down with somebody and say, "Boy, you know, this weather is just really a bummer," and talk things over with people. The guys do. They all bunch up and yak and have their own way of dealing with it, but the women that are in this sort of flying, they are isolated in a sense.

The very first spring that we had Fishing and Flying, we didn't have a lot of extra money, so we went out clam digging and we'd take people out for, say, a seat fare, and then we'd dig clams to make up the rest of the fare and sell the clams. It was a tiny operation at that time. There's not a lot of money in aviation. You do it because you love it. There's no job security here. There are no benefits in little companies. We just eke out a living, but we're proud of what we're doing and like it.

I wouldn't have dreamed of being a pilot. I had been in one airplane in my life. I was just a little farm girl that loved being outdoors. When I was growing up, they weren't the greatest, happiest times. I basically lucked out in some of the things that happened to me, and it was just fortunate that I was restless enough and needed to get some distance between myself and those growing-up years that I came to Alaska, because Alaska and Gayle Ranney really go hand in hand.

Gayle Ranney flying floats in a Piper Super Cub. Cordova, Alaska, 1993.

124

SUZANNE ASBURY-OLIVER

Skywriter *Born September 8, 1958*

Kids are my biggest critics. First- and second-graders are learning how to draw their letters on paper. They'll say, "Well, Mrs. Johnson told us that we start our Ps from the bottom and go up, and you started yours from the middle." I'm not starting in the right places usually is what they say. We've done script, and it's fun to do. Skywriting is always upside down to somebody, somebody's always on the wrong side of it. And if script is upside down to you, it's real hard to decipher. The block letters stay legible longer. As they start to dissipate, you can still kind of read it. Every time you go to do a new word, it's kind of an experiment, testing the water. Once you've done a word, you can perfect it and figure out the easiest way to get through the letters and the quickest way.

When they were skywriting a lot back in the thirties and forties, they were very, very, very secretive about the whole business, because it was so competitive. There were a whole bunch of people doing it, and the edge a skywriter would have would be how much smoke he put out, how long the letters lasted, and how good it looked. If we ever got out of the skywriting business, we would train somebody just the same way we were trained, teach them all of our secrets, and let them have at it. But for now they're like trade secrets.

I guess the most embarrassing thing for a skywriter is to run out of smoke. It's kind of tough. I got about halfway through Pepsi once and ran out, because the spray nozzle had burned off and so it was just allowing a lot more of the fluid to go in. I had no way of knowing that I was going through it faster than I normally do. So I got just like a P and an E up. Then I roll into the next P and nothing's happening. It's like, "Oh, Jesus."

We always say we're off to join the circus, because there's a

....

Suzanne Asbury-Oliver in the cockpit of the 1929 Travel Air D4D open cockpit biplane skywriting for Pepsi over Myrtle Beach, South Carolina, 1994.

Suzanne Asbury-Oliver became a skywriter for Pepsi-Cola Company in 1980. She flies the company's 1929 Travel Air D4D open cockpit biplane that has been used for skywriting advertising by Pepsi since the 1930s. With letters a mile high written across a ten-mile slate of sky, the messages she writes can be seen twenty miles in either direction. Asbury-Oliver learned to fly gliders when she was fourteen years old and became a flight instructor four years later. She met her husband, an aerobatic pilot and airplane mechanic, while flying at air shows for Pepsi. Together they fly as the Pepsi Aerial Entertainers.

Suzanne Asbury-Oliver holding the propeller of the Travel Air D4D at the Marine Corps Air Station New River air show. Jacksonville, North Carolina, 1994.

small group of people that actually make their living doing air shows. It's, I guess, like what rock stars have or circuses have where it's all the preparation and then the show lasts two hours, and then it's over and then you tear it all down and you move on to the next show. So it's kind of a letdown at the end of the weekend, but it's also a relief. You got your job done, and it's time to go to the next spot.

We do about thirty major cities a year. We started out with Steve and me and our "child," which was our dog, traveling just in the biplane. So it was tools, bags, dog, and me in the front seat. For nine months out of the year, that was how we got around. . . . Then we decided a motor home would be better. It makes it possible to live on the road for nine months. We say the traveling is the worst and the best part of the job. It's the thing that makes our life the most difficult by moving every three or four days. But it is what keeps it interesting. If we worked in the same place every weekend, it would be a lot easier, but it also loses some of the fun and the never knowing how things are going to be done. Holidays get pretty much ignored. All of a sudden somebody will say something like, "It's Easter." And we'll say, "Oh, really? We hadn't noticed." It's kind of bad in that way. But it seems like we're always on the road for everything except Christmas. People say, "Do you get tired of this?" And I don't get tired of this, I get tired, just physically, by the end of the season.

We do a lot of small towns where there may not be anything else going on at the airport. I'll be there skywriting, for a Fourth of July festival or whatever. I'll land and there will be thirty or forty people at the fence at the airport just to see the biplane land. It brings back a type of flying that just isn't around very much. They get to see a little bit of the old barnstorming-type flying and the old nostalgic-type skywriting. It's keeping an art form alive that otherwise the majority of the population would never get to see.

When I first started, I thought, "Oh, this will be fun. Two or three years, get to see the country, get to meet a lot of neat people. Get to fly an antique airplane that's got incredible history, and then get on with my plans, my career plan." What was funny was I thought, too, that if I'm going to all these different airports and stuff, I could check out all the different corporate departments and see who's got nice airplanes and who's got good maintenance and who's hiring and who's not, and who's happy and who's not. I'd just kind of drop in, look around, and it seemed like all the people that were flying corporately were envious of what I was doing. I started thinking, "What's wrong with this picture?"

A lot of these antique airplanes, they flew for ten years when they were new, and then they were put in a barn somewhere and in the last ten years somebody's restored them and got them back to flying condition. But this airplane has been flying every year of its life. Basically since 1931 it's always been working as a skywriter, and it's been licensed to fly every year of its life.

I've had several engine failures and it's just something you plan on all the time. We don't fly over mountains unless we're fol-

129

Suzanne Asbury-Oliver checking the engine oil in the 1929 Travel Air D4D before the Marine Corps Air Station New River air show. Jacksonville, North Carolina, 1994.

lowing an interstate so that we at least have that option. We don't fly over swamps, anything that's nonsurvivable or where you're going to lose the airplane. That's a big consideration to us—not losing the airplane. Most of the airplanes that people use in air shows, if the airplane is completely destroyed, you can buy another one or build another one. But this one with all of its history, you know, we just really don't want to have that happen. And that's one of the reasons we started trailering it, because there are those times when you're over something that's going to destroy the airplane if you have to land on it.

You have to be careful talking about the airplane too close to her, because we have this superstition, and it's founded, because somebody will say, "How's the airplane running? How's it doing?" And if you're within earshot—and we've determined what earshot is with this airplane—and you say, "Fine," guaranteed next flight you're going to have a problem. So we got to joking about this and then determined that it was something weird. I mean, it happens. So if somebody says, "How's the airplane doing?" we don't say anything until we get two hundred yards away. But I talk to her a lot. I ask her to be nice, hang together, get me there, don't break down now, that kind of thing. We have mostly home-maintenance chats.

YVONNE McDERMOTT

Pilot *Born May 5, 1976*

One day my teacher's mother was sick, so a substitute came in for the day. I was talking to my friend, and she said, "Really, you want to be a pilot?" and the substitute heard, so he comes up to me and says, "Well, I'm a pilot." And I asked, "How do I get into it, tell me something about it." And then he told me about the military and this school Embry-Riddle Aeronautical University.

When I got [to Embry-Riddle], it was nothing like I thought it would be, because the flying part isn't the hard part; it's the understanding of everything around you, like the weather. I just thought a cloud was a cotton cloud and I was happy with that, but it's not. You have to know how the engine works. You have to know how high and when you can fly into certain air spaces. They just love to abbreviate everything, so you have to try to figure out these abbreviated words. There's so much to say, but then they shortcut it all.

I was thinking, "How am I going to ever become a commercial pilot?" They said, "This is what you do first. Then you have a choice to do these things." They're making a path for me. It kind of looks to me like little step ways to take to get up to being a commercial pilot. They teach you and then they kind of push you to do it, which makes it a lot easier. At this school they have a lot of things involving commercial airlines. They have co-ops where you go work for the company for a little while. It could be volunteer work or sometimes they pay you. Then you meet people inside the company.

They're really strict on the radios. You have to talk right and know all the identifications. I'd go, "Prescott ground, Riddle 89ER, request taxi to active with alpha," and then they'll probably respond back where to taxi and you'll say, "Will go, 89ER." They constantly test you on it. They make you do a lot of flight plans, how to do weight and balance.

....

Yvonne McDermott sitting in classroom with flight simulators at Embry-Riddle Aeronautical University. Prescott, Arizona, 1995.

Vietnamese American Yvonne McDermott is a student at Embry-Riddle Aeronautical University in Prescott, Arizona, where she is enrolled in their airline program. While in high school she entered Embry-Riddle's summer school program through Upward Bound, a program that encourages students to go to college. Her interest in aviation began from exposure to airline pilots while visiting her divorced parents. She intends to graduate in 1997 with a degree in aeronautical science. McDermott envisions a career as a pilot for a major airline. She was in her freshman year and a new private pilot at the time of the interview.

One day my instructor said, "Okay, you're going to go do your solo," and I'm whimpering, "I'm not ready." I was scared. I was really nervous about it. So I just pretended that he was still there, so I would sit there and I would just talk, like I was talking to him. If someone was listening, they would probably say I'm crazy. Then once I finished, I got out of the plane and there was a crowd of people, and they clapped for me. Then my instructor went in back of me and cut my shirt off. [The ritual after a first solo flight is to cut the tail from your shirt to show that you have flown by the seat of your pants.] It was great.

You can't rely on anyone else when you fly by yourself. You have to depend on yourself and be confident in yourself to do it. Finding your way around, using the VORs and NDBs [navigational aids] is really easy.

Landing is always fun because it's always different. Sometimes you just have a smooth landing, and you're like, "Yes! I greased it!" And then another time you just come in and all of a sudden wind would come and push you off the runway, and then you'd have to come back in and bounce down the runway, and you're, like, "Awww." Learning all the book work is not fun.

I have been in a class where there were forty-eight people and I was the only girl. It was really weird. The most I ever had in a classroom was five girls in a class of thirty, but the majority of the time there's not a lot of girls. One of my classes was with Debbie Harvey, she's one of the [members] of the Ninety-Nines Inc. International Women Pilots. She was teaching us AS-240, which is

135

basic navigation, and at the beginning of each class she always has a current affairs [discussion]. She was just mentioning about how at one time there was this lady who crashed the F-14 plane. She said, "If this was a man who crashed this plane, would it have been on the news and so much publicized?" She was trying to be really open-minded, even though she's pro-women, obviously. But then this one guy, he said, "Well, I don't think she should have ever gotten into a plane. There's no way that women should fly fighter planes, especially because they have PMS and they might be pregnant and stuff like that." She asked the rest of the class and a lot of guys were saying "Oh wow, you're full of it." And they said, "The best thing is to have a bunch of women on PMS just go to another country and fight." Everyone would say, "Kill! Kill! Kill!" It was really funny.

Everything in our house is Vietnamese. We have Buddha stands around. [My mother] says in Vietnamese culture she was born as a tree and I was born as a mountain. I stand out by myself really strong and it's okay if I go far away. My other sisters, she wouldn't let them go because one of them was the soil and the water and they really depended on the tree, which means that they had to stay together. But me, I was the mountain, so she says, "Go away. Have fun."

Ever since we were little, she hasn't babied us; she treated me like an adult from when I was really young. She didn't spoil us in any kind of way, which is good. Not spoiled at all. Everything that we wanted, we pretty much had to go out and do. She was always there to give us money, but on choices and decisions, she would always advise that we make our own decisions, and if they were really bad, she'll bring back one of her old stories, Vietnamese stories. I love listening to those stories. [The stories] have [a lot] to do with our ancestors. We think of how our ancestors are, and then we always kind of stay in that boundary.

She'll always remind us that in Vietnam you don't have a lot of freedom and you don't have a lot of stuff, so you should always see what you have and appreciate it. My grandma is from the South, so the Communists basically took everything that she had. I know when I'm an old lady, I could just imagine sitting there, "Oh, I remember back when I was eighteen and I did my first solo cross-country." I just think that would be really cool.

Studying is really difficult. I'm starting to miss home. I'm afraid that I might not make it. Sometimes I feel that way, but my mom told me that if I really want something, I can work really hard and get it. It's really more a desire than it is anything else. So if you really have a desire and you really fight for it and you keep attacking it, I think I could do it. I really think I can.

Yvonne McDermott seated in the cockpit of an Embry-Riddle Cessna taxiing down the runway. Prescott, Arizona, 1995.

BETTY SKELTON-FRANKMAN

Aerobatic Pioneer *Born June 28, 1926*

I was the kid that would always hang around the airport. Somebody would invite me to go up with them, and, oh, I'd get in any airplane with anybody. After you'd get up, they'd say, "Would you like to try to fly?" and pretty soon you know how to fly. My mother and Dad and I, all three of us started taking lessons at the same time when we formally got into learning, but I'd say a lot of people taught me because so many let me fly their airplanes when I was so young.

Mother had me when she was eighteen and Dad was nineteen. I was the only child, and we just grew up together. We were more like brother and sister. There was a Navy ensign who was instructing us on his time off in Pensacola, Florida. Dad soloed. Mother soloed. One day he took me around the field and came back down and started getting out, and I said, "Oh, are we through?" He said, "No, you're going to go by yourself." And he let me go. After I had gone solo, Dad said, "Don't tell anybody, now, because you're not supposed to, you know. It's not legal."

While I was finishing high school in Tampa, I spent every spare moment at the airport. While my friends were going away to college, I couldn't afford to go to college, so before graduating, I contacted Eastern Airlines and fibbed about my age. I went to work for Eastern Airlines and worked for several years from midnight till eight in the morning so that I could get flying in during the day.

I got into aerobatics quite by accident. The Jaycees in Tampa were putting on an air show for some cause, and they were having a meeting to discuss who was going to fly in the show. Somebody said, "Why don't we get that little girl out at the airport to do some aerobatics?" Dad was at the meeting and he said, "Well, she doesn't know any aerobatics." There was a pilot there who had been an aerobatic pilot in the thirties, and he said, "Oh, I'll teach her some."

Betty Skelton-Frankman with a model of the Curtis Pitts "Little Stinker," the plane she made famous during her career as an aerobatic pilot. Winter Haven, Florida, 1994.

As a young woman Betty Skelton dominated the women's aerobatic field, winning the International Feminine Aerobatic Championship three years in a row, 1948, 1949, and 1950. Performing in both national and international air shows she was famous for the inverted ribbon cut. (The aircraft flies upside down and ten feet off the ground through a ribbon tied between two poles in the ground.) Her airplane, the S-1C Pitts Special, was the smallest aerobatic plane in the world at that time and the second Pitts Special constructed by Curtis Pitts. In 1988 she was inducted into the International Aerobatics Hall of Fame.

So I was *told* I was going to be in the air show. And he taught me how to do a loop and a roll, and that's the only training I've ever had. My first professional air show was in Jacksonville in 1946, and that was the Navy's Blue Angels' very first air show.

When you fly the air show circuit, you're on the road most of the year, and it's hard, especially being based out of Florida. You'd fly for two days to get somewhere, then fly in a show, fly back home again, and practice for three days, and then you're off again. It was a very, very busy life. I handled my own fact sheets, bios, pics, materials, bookings, and advertising — everything. I also wrote a column for *Flying* magazine at the same time. I would keep a little notebook and write it while I was flying, in longhand. I wrote for other aviation publications, too.

When I was doing competitive flying, you had to fly in a box. There were altitude restrictions, as there are now. The primary difference [between then and now] is the equipment. The equipment today is built on the power side. [The planes] will go straight up and just roll till hell freezes over. My feeling on competition was that whether it was a man or a woman you were competing with, the major goal was just to do the very best you could. You were challenging yourself more than you were trying to beat someone else. When I first started aerobatic flying, most people were air show pilots primarily, which we always joked as being "smoke and noise." In other words, go down low and put out a lot of smoke and noise and thrill the crowd. There's a great, great difference in being an air show stunt pilot, so to speak,

140

and an aerobatic pilot, because when you get into aerobatics and particularly competition aerobatics, precision is the key to the success of everything you do.

Aerobatic flying is very dangerous and there are fatalities, and you lose friends. The first one really hits you pretty good and then you become—I guess you build up a barrier to it. I think because I was a woman in that particular time in history, and I had an airplane that would do certain things, men would try to do those same maneuvers and they just couldn't do them with their experience, one or the other. I'm afraid I set up a certain challenge for some of them and I felt badly about that. But that was part of the business.

I've always felt that you make your own luck. There is such a thing as being in the right place at the right time for the right thing, and everybody knows about that. I think you are your own motivator of what happens to you in your life, and if you're fortunate, some people call it luck. Now, when you put it with equipment and dangerous things, I still think that it has to do with the way you meet your challenge. For instance, in flying, I had just a little habit, I had what I called my "A-factor." I figured that if you either keep 10 percent extra altitude or 10 percent extra air speed, most of the time it would save your ass. And it did. When I got in some scrapes, that's what got me out of it, the 10 percent air speed.

I started flying in a Fairchild PT-19, but it wasn't built to fly inverted. We found an old airplane up behind the hangar in Georgia called a 1929 Model Great Lakes 2T1a, and I flew it for about a year and a half until it fell apart. I was in my old 1929 Model Great Lakes, and I looked down and I saw this little teeny-eency airplane and I couldn't believe an airplane could be that small. There were people crowded all around it. I could just hardly wait to get on the ground. At that time Curtis Pitts was with the airplane, I guess, and another man, and I asked if I could sit in it and they said no, I couldn't. As I left, I told myself, "Someday I'm going to own that airplane." I just had to have it. It looked like me. I've always liked little things—little cars. I just fell in love with the airplane. I kept trying to buy it and it changed hands from the builder to an air show promoter. When I heard he was having a little financial problem, as we all did in those days, I called him and he said he knew I'd been wanting it for a long time, and he sold it to me. I had never, ever even sat in the airplane. Most people don't buy airplanes unless they fly them first, but I knew I had to have it. It was exactly what I expected. I spent many hundreds and thousands of hours in that airplane.

I looked after it myself. I was always very careful. I'd do the gassing myself, put in the oil — you know, everything by myself. Because all you have to do is have somebody put the gas cap on crooked and take off and roll over upside down and have the gas in your face one time, and you can't see what you're doing and you've had it. At air shows, I'd have to rope it off because it was so unique and so little that people would just want to swamp it.

You get very attached to a piece of equipment like that, particularly when you've been in some very precarious positions and come out of some tight scrapes. You appreciate the equipment. It's like it's got a life of its own.

I came along, in the eyes of most aviation people if they analyze it, right at the wrong time. I was twenty years too early and twenty years too late. I kind of fell between the cracks. The old barnstorming days were gone. The war came along and these women went into the WASP in the war and I couldn't get in because I wasn't old enough. I fit in the 1948 and 1950s category, when civilian aviation didn't stand for a great deal. I felt at that particular time that there wasn't really a great deal of future for women in aviation, because I could not get on with the airlines, and I couldn't get in the military. There weren't enough competitive aerobatic airplanes to do much in that area except for what I did. If I'd been born twenty years earlier, I would have been racing with Cochran or trying to outdo Amelia Earhart. If I'd been born twenty years later, I'd have been fighting Sally Ride like crazy for that first ride. What could a girl do except go out to some grass field and be a flight instructor the rest of your life? I was a flight instructor, but it was strange. I flew long, long before I could drive a car. It came so natural and so second nature to me that I couldn't understand why people couldn't get in an airplane and do the right thing. I'll soon be seventy, and I can't remember when I couldn't fly.

MICHELE SUMMERS

First Officer *Born July 21, 1968*

"Snorkeler one o'clock," I told the captain. He was like, "Oh, man," because all you see sometimes is this little fluorescent tube sticking out of the water, and it's extremely difficult to see. Everything and everybody is always in your flight path when you want to come in for a landing. Flying floats is much more challenging than wheels to me, because when you land at an airport, you've been cleared to land, and no one else has access to this runway right at that moment but you. On floats, it's a completely different story, especially out here in this marina. It's hilarious to see how all the pilots now hate jet skiers. I've done three go-arounds because of jet skiers. I've come down to a hundred feet off the water and a jet skier will come out of the middle of nowhere.

What is really fantastic to see are the whales. We can't land next to them, but we have circled whales on our sightseeing tours quite often. The person that's the nonflying pilot is the one that does the narration. We'll slow the airplane down and show points of interest, like caves on Norman Island and other British Virgin Islands, old pirate hangouts, and legends that you hear on St. Thomas. Hurricane Louis came. We weathered through it, no problem. Hurricane Marilyn was awful. We were at the control tower, in the hurricane shelter. When we came out the next day, it was amazing. I've never in my whole life seen anything so destructive. We had an airplane down here [from Florida] about two weeks after the hurricane, so we were up and flying after that. The reason we waited so long was that we didn't have a dock in St. Croix, because it was destroyed, so we had to rebuild things. No power, things like that. Trying to figure out how you're going to fuel this airplane. We've got to have generators, to pump up the fuel into the airplane, and fuel was hard to find. After the hur-

....

Michele Summers standing on a float of the DeHaviland Twin Otter in St. Croix, Virgin Islands, 1996.

Michele Summers is a first officer for Seaborne Aviation, a float plane company based in St. Thomas, Virgin Islands, and Ketchikan, Alaska. Typically she flies eight scheduled flights a day carrying passengers between St. Thomas and St. Croix from local downtown docks as well as tourists on sightseeing tours of the U.S. and British Virgin Islands. After graduating with a degree in aeronautical administration, she started her aviation career in the Virgin Islands as a ticket sales agent. Her interest in working for Seaborne Aviation began in 1993, and she soon completed specific training for the company. Summers was promoted to her current position in February 1995.

ricane, everybody was dying to get back and forth to see people, relatives and friends over on the other islands. So, yeah, we were utilized quite a bit, a lot of freight going back and forth, lots of generators.

We started calling St. Thomas the Land of Blue Roofs, because most islanders used to have all red roofs, that was kind of the St. Thomas trademark. Well, now they have FEMA tarps covering everybody's roof. So when you fly, I still prepare everybody, it's nothing but blue. So you see blue sky, blue water, and blue roofs. Everything is blue. Unfortunately, everybody you see down there with a blue roof lost [their real roof].

Typical passengers on the schedule [flights] are usually natives or local business-people, for the most part. A lot of people commute from downtown to downtown so they just get off the dock and walk right up to their office. The thing that drives you nuts, they're always late, and then they complain when you leave them on the dock. When we first started doing the sched, this is just the island life down here, for a 7:00 departure, people—I'm not kidding—would show up at 7:15, 7:30, for a 7:00 departure, and actually expect the airplanes to be there. They would be totally flabbergasted if the airplane was gone on time, and they're like, "Whoa, wait a minute. You're kidding me."

So after a few months of leaving people, they finally got it in their heads, "Oh, this airline leaves on time," and that's like our motto. We're the only airline around here, it seems like, that's on time. Hey, we're not on island time, we're on fixed time. Good points about the people: they're fun to fly because they appreciate what you do, and they like flying on the water.

A lot of people ask me, "So when will you be a pilot? You're in training right now because you're so young?" I say, "No, I'm a full-fledged pilot. I went to the same school that the captain went to," which is true. Then they ask, "Oh, but how old are you?" I look younger, I think, than what I am, twenty-seven, especially because my hair is all pulled back in a ponytail.

My PawPaw, my grandfather, always thought, probably up until the day he died, I was a flight attendant. Every time I'd go visit him, I'd tell him, "I fly airplanes, PawPaw, I don't serve anybody." If I had a dollar for every time I was asked what I was going to serve on this airplane, I'd probably have at least a thousand dollars, easy.

I was the first person on both sides of the family so far that's even graduated college. Nobody was ever interested in aviation, so it was real hard for me to talk about wanting to fly, because nobody understood and nobody could relate to what I was doing or what I was talking about, for God's sake, because aviation is a completely different language, just like being a doctor is.

I have paid for every single one of my flight hours. In fact, for my wedding, my parents offered to pay for a huge wedding. I didn't want all of that. My dad and I were talking one day when he said, "I'm going to give you this amount for your wedding. If you want to use it to do something else and have a small wedding, I'll go along with that." I said, "Cool." So that's how I bought my private ticket [private pilot's license].

Michele Summers after tying the DeHaviland Twin Otter to the dock at St. Croix, Virgin Islands, 1996.

The beauty of this place is great, living down here, and the weather, obviously, is wonderful. It's very easy to lose yourself down here, meaning that life is so slow and so incredibly laid-back that I can see how people just come down here and escape reality. I used to be Little Miss Party Girl, but now that I work twelve-and-a-half-hour days four and five days a week, I don't want to go out. We usually time out between thirty and thirty-four hours a week, and that's all you can fly is thirty-four.

It was easier for me to start flying commercially here in the Caribbean, I think, than in the States. There's less competition, not as many pilots down here. In the States, it seems like the market is flooded, pilots are a dime a dozen. When we first moved down here we took Seaborne's sightseeing tour of the BVI's, and I fell in love with it. I thought "Wow!" This is a beautiful airplane, this is just the life, living in the Caribbean flying on the water. It just seemed so romantic and seemed to all flow together." I kept bugging Chuck, the owner of Seaborne, about flying floats. I'm the second lowest time pilot that the company has, I think that maybe he was giving me a break.

I still say I want to be a pilot when I grow up, because I still can't believe I get paid for this. It just doesn't seem real at the moment. This is too cool. This is what I want.

Michele Summers looking out of the cockpit window for clearance as the DeHaviland Twin Otter departs from a floating dock in St. Thomas, Virgin Islands, 1996.

TROY DEVINE

Captain, United States Air Force *Born March 28, 1962*

My heart is ripped right out of me when crises develop and I have any inclination that we're going to deploy there. When something happens anywhere in the world, it's the job of our program to be ready to respond and provide information to theater commanders. All I want, my whole focus of life, is to go and deploy on the contingency operations. The threats that are involved in a situation like that are usually numerous, but I still can't stop myself for wanting to do that more than anything. I want to be there with the first group that goes in.

I have logged combat sorties, I have flown in combat areas. We continue to do that on a daily basis in the same theaters where every other platform is logged in combat time. We cannot deliver weapons. However, many weapons in every theater we fly are pointing at us, so I think the definition of what a combat pilot is, I mean, if you are in a combat theater and you are engaging in that theater's primary role, then you're a combat pilot.

When you go into different theaters, you're fully briefed through the intelligence channels on what threats are out there. It's not like it's a surprise. Occasionally it's disturbing when you get locked up, for instance, in a target track and radar is looking at you. However, we're trained. I have a lot of confidence in the other support aircraft that are in the field. No matter how uncomfortable I feel about it at the time, I know that I'm either going to go up there and I'm going to collect the information that we need to get that day, or somebody else is going to have to. So it might as well be me. I like doing it. It's my job.

We're exposed to cabin altitudes of about 28,000 feet, which is uncomfortable for long periods of time. If we had a rapid decompression above 60,000 feet, we would be killed, because the pressures on our bodies are not adequate to keep our blood liquid, and it would

Captain Troy Devine, USAF, seated in the cockpit of a Lockheed U-2R. Beale Air Force Base, Beale, California, 1995.

Troy Devine is the first female Captain in the history of the U.S. Air Force U-2 program. She flies the Lockheed U-2R on classified reconaissance "spy" missions over battle areas throughout the world. The U-2R is a difficult aircraft to fly due to its long wings allowing for unusual landing characteristics. Devine's assignments often keep her away from home for two months at a time. She has also flown research missions to collect scientific data from air sampling flights, land management and crop estimates for the Department of Agriculture, and flood and earthquake damage assessments. Devine is married to a U-2 Captain and has a baby boy.

try to boil out—and obviously that would ruin our day! So as a backup to the pressurization system, we wear a full-pressure suit and breathe 100 percent oxygen at all times.

Now you're completely sealed off in a pressure suit, breathing 100 percent oxygen. So eating and drinking and doing the things that happen after you eat and drink become a problem at that point. The way they've come around that is they have tube food, which is just pureed foods of different varieties, and being a quasi-vegetarian myself, I stick to the fruits. Then we bring bottles with long tubes that you can stick through a food port to either eat or drink through, and that's how we drink. For my entire time in this program flying operationally, I wore a large diaper, but that's designed to take urine away, not anything else. So diet control is very important the day before and the day of your flight. You eat foods that are high in protein and low in residue so that you can kind of regulate your biological requirements for that.

The bread and butter of the operational flying is a nine-hour sortie. You have to find ways to allow yourself to accept the fact that you're going to be strapped into an ejection seat at altitude for quite a long time. You try not to dwell on the actual hours that are going by, but you occupy each hour [with] almost a ritualistic "Over this hour, these are the things that I'm going to accomplish," and do it in a methodical manner so that you don't get yourself in a fur ball of "Now I've done everything and I still got four hours to go. I'm going to lose my mind." People expect you, as a U-2 pilot, to go out there, do your mission,

Captain Troy Devine, USAF, seated on the wing (total wingspan 103 feet) of a Lockheed U-2R in a full-pressure suit. Beale Air Force Base, Beale, California, 1995.

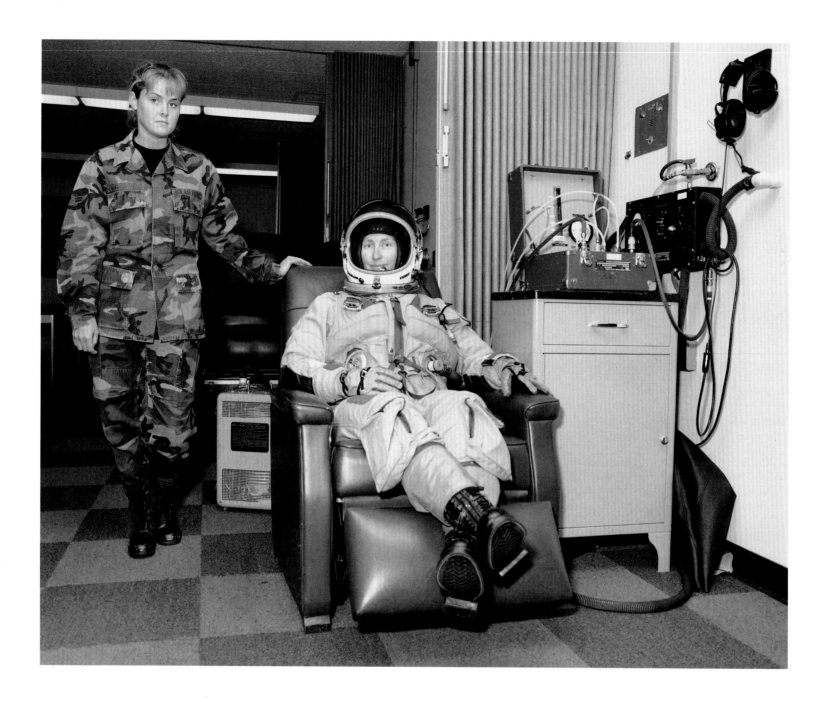

come back, land an airplane that's very difficult to land, protect the national resource by flying it well in all phases of flight, and not make yourself an international incident. So navigational errors are not acceptable. Mechanical malfunctions obviously happen, but we fully expect in our community that you as a pilot are going to do whatever you need to do [to avoid putting] yourself or this program in an awkward situation.

Every single landing, regardless of your level of expertise, requires all of your concentration. Through the history of the program, that struggle with the airplane in the landing phase, that's where the nickname the Dragon Lady has come from. It could be on a day where it seems very benign out there, the runway environment is favorable, and you could still have problems in the landing phase. So it requires all of your concentration to land the airplane, especially after long missions and in the pressure suit, but anytime you land it, you've got to give it a lot of respect. I remember my first couple of landings in the U-2 feeling absolutely like I was flailing, and I remember halfway through my second interview sortie, the feeling that the "light went on" and I understand this dance with this airplane.

Women were not accepted into the program before I interviewed. I think there was some resistance to having women in the program—not conceptually so much as logistically. The thing that stuck out in my mind was, if they did have problems with it, after the interview process was over and I flew and passed and the program selected me, that was the end of it. I never felt, even once, any resistance from that point forward. The only thing that I felt from the other brothers in the community was a strong sense of support and belonging.

In a perfect world, the fact that I'm pregnant and I'm going to have a baby would never enter into anything that happens at work. I would never talk about it until it became totally obvious. But because I have to be grounded to continue with the pregnancy, obviously, there was a point where I have to say, "Hey, I can't fly anymore because I'm pregnant." For me, I found that very awkward. Because I was the first woman in this unit, I've done everything I could to not be different, and it wasn't hard because my focus here is to be an aviator, not to be a woman aviator, just to be a good pilot. I've tried to earn respect on that basis, and this is the first time in my career as a U-2 pilot where it is painfully obvious that I'm not like everybody else.

As soon as the flight surgeon realizes you're pregnant, you're grounded. It's hard on me not to fly, it's all I've ever done in the Air Force. That's an ejection seat. That's Air Force policy.

Now that I'm going on to a staff job where I won't be flying and I won't be around the community, I know that any day or night when I wake up, somewhere in the world, one of my brothers in the program—or sisters, as it is now—will be on station in some location in the world where he is in peril and he is doing his job in an arduous mission, and bringing critical information back.

·····························

Troy Devine waits for her flight suit to pressurize with oxygen. Beale Air Force Base, Beale, California, 1995.

EVIE WASHINGTON

Pilot *Born March 27, 1946*

I was given to my grandparents when I was three days old, and I stayed with them until I graduated from high school. My grandfather had a large farm out in the country, and I grew up working the fields and driving the trucks. He taught me how to shoot a rifle. Of course, that used to knock me off the fence into the pigpen. When you live in the South, you do a lot of things much earlier, because you have nobody out there, no real laws to say that you can't do it. You drive at the age of nine.

We were only thirty miles from the state of Mississippi, and there's a military base in Columbus. Being so close, C-130 and C-141 airplanes came across our field real low. I guess I was around nine, ten years old. I just knew that it was something different, it was faster than cars, and I wanted to do it. When I was growing up, I did not know anything about any pilots. I didn't know anything about the Tuskegee Airmen or Bessie Coleman or Amelia Earhart. Ironically, the Tuskegee Airmen trained in Tuskegee, which is in Alabama, about two and a half hours' drive to the south, but I didn't know anything about them at that time. Flying was just what I wanted to do.

I graduated from high school in May of 1964, and I told my grandfather I wanted to go to an airline school. My grandfather never did think that there wasn't anything that a girl couldn't do or that she shouldn't do. You would think someone his age would think that a girl's place was in the home. But that wasn't his idea. He always told me that anything that most men had, I could have myself if I worked hard enough for it.

I got an interview with an airline to be a flight attendant. They wanted me to weigh 115 pounds when they hired me because the Vietnam War was going on and they had the contract to fly the wounded back and forth from Vietnam. I was weighing at that time

Evie Washington at Hyde Field, the airport where she learned to fly in 1984. Clinton, Maryland, 1995.

Evie Washington gives flight instruction and is a Cadet Flight Orientation pilot for the Civil Air Patrol. Devoting her time and aircraft fees to "Opportunity Skyway," she introduces children to aviation careers by giving orientation flights and lectures at airports and schools. While financially supporting her nephew's flight lessons, she has furthered her own education with a master of arts degree and several airplane ratings: her latest being an Airline Transport Pilot license, which she needs to pursue her goal to work for the airlines. Currently she is working on a book for children about African Americans in aviation.

87 pounds. They gave me six months to get fat. Everybody was telling me how to get fat. I was to the point by the end of six months I just couldn't even stand to see food again, and I only gained like three pounds out of all of that. I only gained weight about twenty years later.

I tried to go into the Air Force. At that time, they didn't accept women pilots. They didn't even have that many black pilots, period. They tried to push me off into doing like clerical stuff and I said, "That's not what I want to do. If I can't fly, there's no way I'm going to come in here and go through boot camp and suffer doing push-ups and running, to do these little frilly jobs." So I didn't go in.

Not being able to go into the military, I decided I'd just prepare myself and make some money. So I continued with going to night school. I made up my mind that once I finished my degrees, I was going to go back to school and learn how to fly.

The night before my check ride [for a private pilot's license], I was so nervous I ended up vomiting. It was raining, and I kept thinking, "Oh, goodie, I won't have to take this check ride." I could put it off and then go back up for some more instructions. By daybreak, the rain had stopped. All the instructors kept saying, "If you flunk this check ride, you have nothing to blame it on but yourself. You can't blame it on the wind." I mean, the wind was dead calm. And that made me even more nervous.

He [FAA flight examiner] wanted me to do an emergency landing, as if the engine had gone out. So he closed the throttle, and I was supposed to set the best glide and circle

around and land. They usually let you get down to about five hundred feet off the ground. So I found this nice field that was well plowed and everything. I set it up perfect. Then he said, "Okay, let's go." The minute I pushed the throttle forward to give me full power and pulled back on the control wheel to climb, my seat went flying back— ZOOM! I go, "Oh, gosh, this is it. This is the pink slip." He didn't say anything. He looked at me and I looked at him. I said, "You want the airplane?" He said, "What would you do if you were flying by yourself?" My feet couldn't even get the rudders at that time because my seat was too far back, but I could reach over and trim the airplane down out of the climb that I had it in, and I knew if I let it continue to climb it was going to stall out. So I trimmed it down pretty level, and reached down and pulled my seat up and locked it. Once I got my seat up, got everything back into position, he looked at me and said, "That was very good. Most students panic. I have to take over, but you did it all by yourself. That was really good." I said, "Oh God, I got through that one."

We came back and did some landings. He got out, and he didn't say anything. And I thought, "Oh, gosh, I've done something wrong." The guys came and they said, "Boy, you've really done it. We told you, you didn't have anybody to blame but yourself." I thought, "Oh, God, I didn't pass. I didn't pass." At that time, Bob Jenkins [FAA examiner] came out, and he had on this big smile and this white piece of paper in his hand. He said, "Congratulations!" And the guys just roared. They laughed. "We got you. We got

Evie Washington at Hyde Field. Clinton, Maryland, 1995.

you." I was ready to beat them up. That was the best feeling I ever had because a lot of people don't pass the check ride their first time around.

Sometimes people tell you, "You just don't know what you want to do. You've got a degree in psychology and you've got a [master's] degree in business and now you're taking flying." It's as if they think your brain is going to work on one wavelength. Every now and then you get a few people that ask you why you want to be up there or you get some people that would ask, "Can you control the airplane?" Their perception of being able to fly is being something really masculine, as if you've got to really use force. And you tell them you can pretty much control the airplane with just the tip of your little finger. It doesn't require much pressure. But they mainly look at the airplane: "How can you do it?"

Flying itself is very expensive, and most of the time you do not, especially black women, get the support of family and friends. You get more discouragement than anything. Of course, with my being single, it was easier, because I didn't have anybody tell[ing] me how to spend my money. No, I had people tell[ing] me how to spend my money. Although it wasn't their money, they told me I was crazy to spend it on flying. You can learn something from the criticism and discouragement that people offer you, and at times if you look at it in an objective way, it can be a motivating force for you.

BONNIE WILKENS

Helicopter Pilot *Born April 14, 1961*

Smokey is fictitious, although you probably don't realize he's not a real bear. Smokey represents an image of a savior, educating people to be careful and not start fires. He's there to say, "Don't light fires. Be careful with matches. We want to preserve the forest, and once it's gone it's gone." Whereas my whole function is not to prevent anything, but to prevent it from getting bigger. So I would have to say that I don't really feel like I'm Smokey. I'm kind of an assistant, if you like.

Dropping water—it's just so much fun. There's so many ways you can drop. You can hover or you can descend momentarily and drop and it gives more force to the water. You can trail drop where you have a small amount of speed. You can turn and drop at the same time, which gives you a wider arc in a circular pattern. Every drop is different, it just depends on where it's wanted and what the fire is doing.

When you hit the trigger, almost instantaneously it's coupled with the water being released from the helicopter, and the helicopter gets really light and it starts to rise up because you've released 800 pounds' worth of load from the bottom of it. But really, hitting the button isn't what excites me. It's looking out the door and watching the water sort of being like a magnet and going right to the flames, and out goes the fire.

The most publicized fire I have been on was the Santa Barbara fire, which burnt six hundred homes. That was kind of a big, quick fire, and it was all over in three days. In California, quite often there is nothing [no water source], so you just take what you can get. I try not to use swimming pools until I don't have anything else to use. If their house is in jeopardy, they love you. But if they think the fire is far enough away, It's like, "I don't want you dipping out of my pool,

....

Bonnie Wilkens at helibase with a Bell 206 B-III Jet Ranger with an attached "Bambi" bucket. Mount Pocono, Stroudsburg, Pennsylvania, 1994.

Bonnie Wilkens has worked as a helicopter pilot since 1984. Her work includes agricultural spraying, controlled burning, and fire suppression. To put out fires she can drop one hundred gallons of water with a collapsible "Bambi" bucket attached to the bottom of the helicopter. She grew up in England and attended an all-boys school for her secondary education, where she learned how to parachute jump. She was one of twenty people selected to attend the Cranfield Institute of Technology, in England, where she obtained her master's degree in bioaeronautics. Later she came to Agrotors in Pennsylvania for her helicopter training.

can't you use somebody else's pool?" But if it is absolutely the only water source, you are allowed to use it. If you use a pool you have to be careful that you don't blow the plastic lawn furniture through the front glass window or something.

I've used the ocean before. The day I used the ocean there were six-foot swells. That was hard because in order that the waves wouldn't hit my skids, I would have to go out and down just to throw my bucket because the waves would come in and down. Usually we try to get two-minute turnarounds, every two minutes you are dipping another bucket full. In the course of an hour you've done like thirty drops at a hundred gallons a drop, which is quite a lot of water.

When you first get to a fire, sometimes there's no landing area which has been prepared, so you have to basically take whatever you can get. And if it means coming down through a hole vertically [between the trees] and you have to take each person in one at a time so that the aircraft isn't heavy, to deliver them to a fire safely, then that's how you have to do it. Sometimes we have to land in a pre-burn area, so you come in and make a water drop, "dust abate" is what it's called. Once it's dust-abated, then you can come in and land, you don't suck all the ashes back down into the intake of the engine.

When I first started flying on the West Coast, nobody ever talked to me on the radio. I'd get there, and they'd send me to, say, Division G, and I'd call this Division G supervisor on the radio and they wouldn't call me back. They just wouldn't answer. I'd get tired. I'd just keep saying, "Division G,

this is 140. This is helicopter 140. This is the helicopter overhead." Eventually, somebody would go, "Are you in the helicopter? Oh, we didn't know that was you. We thought you were in dispatch or you were working down at the helibase." In terms of [heli-tack pilots], I've never bumped into any women.

Controlled burning, the intentional setting fire to things, is unbelievable fun. You have a drip torch, which uses gelled fuel. You can write your name with that stuff. It's basically napalm, although they don't really like to say that's what you are using. It's a gelled fuel and it's an external load, which hangs under the helicopter about twelve to fifteen feet. As soon as that stuff hits the ground, it starts to burn. If you're a pyromaniac, it's just incredible, because when you hit that button you can see all these flames. It's instant gratification.

Just like when you drop water, as soon as you drop it, it puts the fire out. So it's kind of a flip-flop. You're burning out all the debris, the rubble, nettles, and brambles, and it releases the nutrients back into the ground, and removes any competitive plants. But it's potentially a super-dangerous thing. You have to be careful that you don't [un]intentionally burn somebody else's property or neighboring crops, obvious considerations. There's a lot of precision flying. You can't be sloppy. You have to put that stuff within a foot of where it needs to be. You have to know a lot about fire behavior; if you didn't, almost for sure you'd burn down somebody's home or something.

I really like spraying because, for one, I got my master's degree in it. I like the whole concept of it. I like the long days. It's worth-while in the sense that you're treating pests which, if they got to epidemic levels, could just be horrible. If you've really ever seen defoliation from gypsy moths, it's extreme. The spraying is fun. You can legally hot-dog around, although it's in no way hard on the aircraft. It's the perception of figuring out how you're going to do the field, making sure the chemical runs out at the right time and that everything's treated properly. You're not just haphazardly flying around all over the place.

I may go from here to Alaska or from here to Florida or wherever, so I pack for basically any weather situation, because I may not go home. I live mostly in motels. The good thing is I never have to do any housework. I never have to make the bed, another big plus. And it's clean and tidy and all that good stuff.

We [my husband (also a heli-tack pilot) and I] usually go our separate ways but often end up on the same fires or we've been on contracts at the same base or close to each other. And [at] the other extreme there are some times where I'm in Arizona and he's in Maine. That's just the way it goes.

DOROTHY AIKSNORAS-VALLEE

First Officer *Born September 16, 1949*

I used to always carry around a "co-puppet" because I always thought, well, if something goes wrong, you don't blame yourself. I'd blame it on the puppet. One day I was down in Florida for Sun and Fun [annual air show]. I was flying down the coast. I was real low and I saw a train. I went and buzzed the train and I saw the engineer. So as I came back to fly next to him, I took out my puppet and did one of these [waves the puppet]. There's an open cockpit. So the guy saw it and I took off. I came around again, came by to give him another one [wave], and I had my puppet out doing it. And you know what? He had the same puppet. He was giving me one back.

I started flying in my sophomore year [of college]. I was sitting in the Student Union one day and this fellow walked by me and he said, "Hey, I'm going up for a flight lesson, flying. Wanna come?" I didn't know him other than seeing him playing the guitar at the coffeehouse every Friday night. I was sitting in the back of the airplane. He was flying. I was looking around thinking, "This is it!"

I was the first girl to get their pilot's license at the Oxford, Connecticut, Airport. I spent all my days up at the airport. I cleaned airplanes and I worked with mechanics, helped them change the oil and tires. I fell in love with a guy. He was a well-known aerobatic pilot, and I helped him work on his airplane. He used to go down to Texas every year for the aerobatic nationals. One year I followed him down to go and help him and while I was down there I ran into Paul Poberezny, the founder of the Experimental Aircraft Association (EAA) Museum. He watched me work on his airplane and then invited me up to Wisconsin. He offered me a job as a secretary, and I told him I really wanted to be a mechanic. So I went and became an apprentice. I learned how to do welding, fabric work, I learned how to paint an airplane. [When building an

Dorothy Aiksnoras-Vallee standing in the engine turbine of a Boeing 757 after checking the airplane over as part of her pre-flight duties as first officer for Northwest Airlines. National Airport, Washington, D.C., 1993.

Dorothy Aiksnoras-Vallee is a first officer for Northwest Airlines, flying Boeing 757s. Entering the commercial airline industry as a mechanic in 1979, she upgraded to a pilot four months later. She was one of the first licensed female aircraft and powerplant (referred to as A&P) mechanics to restore, build, and paint several aircraft at the Experimental Aircraft Association (EAA) Museum in Oshkosh, Wisconsin. She has built two of her own aircraft: an Acro Sport and a Christen Eagle II. Currently she is raising her two sons as a single parent.

airplane from scratch] my boss, he taught me never to look at the big picture. One step at a time. Come in and think about one little piece that you've got to have done. It's going to be shining in the airplane by the end of the day. He said, "Remember all those little pieces after the whole year, there's 365 of them. Put it all together, the piece gets bigger and larger and larger." And that's how I learned to do it. You learn patience. You apply it to a lot of things in life.

I didn't have any person that was a role model. When I went to the airport as a teenager, I suppose I just did things that I wanted to do. And whether the person doing it was—they were all men, that was fine with me.

I don't know too many women who have their mechanic's ratings. I bet you on one hand I can count how many women have built their own airplanes. I always thought that the building took a heck of a lot more perseverance and just determined what kind of person you really were, rather than the flying. Any monkey could fly an airplane. I didn't really think about being an airline pilot until probably around the end of 1977, the beginning of 1978, and then I started full bore sending out résumés to everybody I could think of. Spring of 1979, I got hired on by Pilgrim Airlines, but I was a mechanic first. They wouldn't let me be a pilot. I was a mechanic for them for four or five months before they let me be a pilot.

The best part about flying is that every day I fly I can probably be guaranteed that it's going to be a sunny office. And watching sunsets and the Northern Lights. It looks like a shimmering curtain of different greens and bright colors, dropped on a stage, and it's like somebody has a fan behind the curtain that keeps moving back and forth and dancing in the sky. And sunrises, You've got to look real closely on a sunrise to catch that green light. Not too many people see the green. It only lasts thirty seconds or so. So we really do have a good seat up there.

It only happens once in a blue moon, when you're flying right on top of a cloud deck and the sun is just coming over the cloud deck, you can see the clouds going by because you're just above them. You can tell how fast you are going. Usually you're doing about 435 knots, 500 miles an hour. That's pretty fast. At 23,000 feet that really makes you think about where all this stuff comes from. You can transform yourself about: Where do these clouds come from? Where does this whole life come from? What is life all about? All these questions go through your head so fast. And that's kind of a neat feeling.

You don't let yourself get into a position of complacency. That's very easy in this cockpit because it's all computerized and the airplane will do whatever you programmed it to do, and if you don't pay attention to it, it'll take you somewhere where you wonder where the heck you're going. You can program everything in the airplane. The captain has to taxi out to the end of the runway, push the power levers up, click a little button. Now the pilot levers are all on automatic. Pull the airplane off. Click everything on. Pull up the gear. Pull up the flaps. And the airplane now will climb all the way up to wherever you tell the program to go, level off, go right where you have it programmed to go. It will land. It will stop at the end of the runway where you have it programmed. We use the program as a backup, but we don't usually make the airplane do all of it automatically, only because you want to keep your flying skills.

I'm not a real extrovert. But now since the world is changing and our airline is suffering a little bit, I thought if I could just make one person want to fly us again it helps my paycheck. If I'm getting on the airplane and I see people sitting around, I'll maybe stop and say hello to them. I'll tell them what the weather's going to be like where we're going. Or I'll help a mom out. After every flight now I get out from the cockpit if I flew the leg, to say goodbye to everyone and "Thank you for choosing Northwest" and more than 95 percent of the time, if the other pilot is behind me, the people look at me and just look right through me to him and ignore me. They think I'm the flight attendant or maybe I'm the jetway operator. I've learned to laugh at it, well, maybe I'm a ghost today that you can't see.

I'll give you my typical week. Sunday I get up and I go to church and we have all day off. Monday, bring the kids to school, pick them up. Monday night, go swimming. Tuesday, get up, bring the kids to school, go to Bible study. Get packed. Leave by Tuesday afternoon. Get out to Detroit at seven o'clock at night or five o'clock at night. Go do my runaround. Get in the airplane. Fly off to San Francisco or whatever, stay overnight. Wednesday, get up, fly coast to coast, stay overnight in Boston. Thursday morning, get up, fly Boston back to Minneapolis, back to Detroit by 7:30 at night. Get on an 8:30 flight, fly back to Connecticut. Get home by 11:30, quarter to 12:00 at night. That's Tuesday, Wednesday, Thursday. Friday morning, get up, bring the kids to school, pick them up at 3:30. Friday night go to swimming. Saturday morning, get up at 7:00, bring the kids to music lessons, have the rest of the day off. And then we're back at Sunday again. And in the meantime I have to make sure I get all the laundry done, make sure when I'm going to go to work, I can tell my parents who's going to pick up the kids and what's going to happen, and keep up with their money thing. Make sure all my bills get paid. And when the summer comes, just try to keep the motor home going, and keep the airplane going.

My eight-year-old thinks I'm only going to work for a couple more years and then Mom's going to be home all the time. He's wishing that I was home all the time. I can imagine. Kids need Mom home. Oh, it's hard. It's hard on all of us. But it's a means to an end.

MARILYN BRIDGES

Aerial Photographer *Born December 26, 1948*

As a child, I used to make drawings in the earth, and I believed that rocks were magical. And now, years later here I am photographing the prehistoric markings of Nazca, Peru, and other earthworks around the world. My interest seems to have been continuous when I think about it.

When I was in Peru, the only way I could see the gigantic earth drawings of Nazca was to go up in a small plane. They removed the door, and I was very, very frightened because I had never been in a small plane before, and not only was I in this small plane but the door was off. I felt sick to my stomach and I went through every emotion you can imagine that might stop a person from flying. But what I was looking at was so miraculous! The Lines of Nazca are incredible; they cover about eighty square miles and are visible only from above.

My first photographs of Nazca didn't turn out well because I didn't know how to shoot from the air. But I was so excited by what I saw, I wanted to share it with other people. So I went back to the United States and figured out how to make a good aerial photograph, what shutter speed to use, what film, what kind of filters. Then I went back to Peru and photographed again and that work was very successful. I was also able to give the work a feeling: it wasn't just documentary photography, it had a feeling, a "longing for the past."

When I started looking for more places to photograph, I found that money was a problem because it was very expensive to hire planes. So I started to apply for grants and the first grant I got was a Guggenheim. Once I got the Guggenheim I knew that I could pursue my work.

In a way I'm a visual anthropologist because I see the structure of

....

Marilyn Bridges holding one of the cameras she uses for aerial photography. Warwick, New York, 1995.

Fine art photographer Marilyn Bridges travels around the world photographing landscapes from small airplanes. Her photographs depict the markings in the earth that have been left behind both by ancient cultures and by contemporary society. Bridges received her master's degree in fine art photography at the Rochester Institute of Technology and has received numerous awards including a Guggenheim Fellowship, a Fulbright Grant, and a National Endowment for the Arts Grant. Her photographs are currently on exhibit worldwide and her most recent publication is *Egypt: Antiquities from Above*.

the archaeological sites and the way that they were placed by man within the landscape. I can show people a view of what's here on the planet that they can't see in normal life. We all walk around and look with a perpendicular viewpoint—we look at things from the front and the back and from alongside. And here I am looking down from above at the juxtaposition of man's markings and the natural landscape, observing the traces left on the earth's surface.

I fly at the edge of stall speed. Often the warning buzzer will go off. I also love to fly four to five hundred feet off the ground. I don't want to get so low, though, that it almost looks like you're standing on a ladder rather than being up in the air. I always want to convey that feeling of flying.

I watch the light of the day as if I were in a studio. I watch how the sun shines on the subject I'm shooting. I might want raking, dark heavy shadows behind a rock formation for instance, or recently I've been doing a lot more back lighting, where I use the wing of the plane as the lens shade. Especially for water shots, that can be really beautiful. I can't control the images but I can control what I do. I can control the way I hold the camera, the angle I hold the camera at, the way I ask to have the plane to perform, with a certain type of bank or certain level of altitude.

I won't shoot through glass because I want everything sharp. When I was photographing Machu Picchu, Peru, they had to remove the rear cargo door and a friend of mine held my ankles as I hung out of the plane. That was the best! We were up so high

in altitude, that I might have been feeling a little bit of "grandeur" from lack of oxygen. I felt just like a condor hovering over Machu Picchu. There I was, flying within the tips of the Andes Mountains, and I didn't want to stop. Sometimes I'm totally fearless that way. Whatever part of the plane I can open up, I'll shoot out of it as long as the wing isn't in the way.

I didn't learn to fly until I went down to the Yucatán in a small plane with a pilot friend of mine. Neither one of us spoke Spanish, and when we got down there we were lost. I wasn't a pilot yet; I was just a photographer. And my friend said, "Marilyn, you have to take the controls and fly this plane because I have to put all my energy into the navigation." And I thought, "Oh great —I put my trust in this person to bring me here, and now we are lost and I have to fly the plane." And I started flying the plane and I really enjoyed it. After that experience, I decided to get my pilot's license immediately.

When you're involved in this kind of work, you really need to know how a plane flies and what its limitations are: how slow you can go, how low, what kind of turns and banks. Then there's also a pilot language. I used to just say, "I want to fly low." Or "I don't understand why I can't fly over there," and it might have been a controlled airspace, but I wasn't aware of it. Before I was a pilot, I was made fun of at the airports. They'd see this attractive woman with all of these heavy cameras, and I had little understanding about aviation. I was a perfect target, in a way, for ridicule. And once I got my pilot's license, everything changed. It became so much easier and so much safer too.

Now I can make a judgment about the pilot. Before I got my license I didn't know who I was flying with, and sometimes I would feel that the plane was just not being handled right, but if anything happened I wasn't sure what in the world I could do. Just as I need to be aware of how a camera works, how an aperture works with the shutter speed and how the focus works on a camera, I really need to understand how the plane can fly. And when I want a certain angle for my photograph, I need to know I can get it, and if I'm asking too much or too little. And now I'm enlightened as to exactly how much I can ask.

I think people really don't know how to take me. I think I'm strange to them because I do this kind of work and I travel so much. I'm traveling almost all of the time. I'm doing something most women wouldn't do alone— going to countries like Egypt and Peru, and then on top of that I hang out of airplanes. It's not easy.

I've never had to do an emergency landing and I've never crashed, but unfortunately three pilots I have flown with have crashed and died, two in Peru due to mechanical failure, a month or two after I'd been flying with them, and the other in Nevada because of pilot error. It's very sad, and when someone dies up there, it makes you realize that this isn't anything to fool around with.

The ultimate satisfaction is to share my vision of what I've seen of the earth from that altitude and to have the work recognized for both its historical content and its artistic style. My work has been shown at art museums—the Museum of Modern Art, in New York, and the Bibliothèque Nationale in Paris—as well as historical institutions, such as the Museum of Natural History and the Smithsonian. It's also been published and exhibited throughout the world.

I think flying is satisfying to me as a woman because it has developed my strength. Being a creative personality, I had to develop the discipline of technique and a mastery of the mechanics as well. That was a side of me that I had never developed. It taught me to become strong as far as traveling and working with other people, and going into a male-dominated world. It's given me a sense of myself that I wouldn't have explored if I had ended up in another career. And it helped me to see the planet and to understand humankind through flying and photography.

As far as what the future holds, I think the future is an accumulation of the present and I'm trying to be as present as possible in my work and what I'm doing—I'm loving it. Even though sometimes it's strenuous physically and mentally, the rewards are far greater than the part that hurts. My images now are, I think, the best that I've done. And I don't want to lose it. It's not something you can take a long vacation from. Artistically, when you feel something is really working within, you have to keep the flow going.

DORIS LOCKNESS

Flying Octogenarian *Born February 2, 1910*

When I flew "Swamp Angel" [Vultee Stinson L-5 with a 190 horsepower Lycoming engine that served in New Guinea in World War II] to the air shows, I knew exactly what the first two questions would be. "Did you fly that plane in here by yourself?" And I'd say yes. And the next question was "How old are you?" They just looked amazed. I had a couple of ladies say, "Gee, I dropped my license at about fifty. If you can fly that, I'm going to go out and get my license in force again." So, I run into a lot of instances like that, I think I inspired people along the way quite a little bit. The prerequisites to be a United Flying Octogenarian—you must be actively flying at age eighty, and have a medical and a biannual flight review, and be able to be pilot in command.

I was twenty-nine years old when I started to fly, and that's because I had moved close to a small airport. I noticed these little planes flying close to our house so I just had to go over there and look at them. I just thought, well, gee, I'd like to fly one of those airplanes; that's all there was to it. So when I got the youngsters off to school, and that would be the fastest housework you've ever seen done, I rode a bicycle over to the airport. The flying time, to begin, for a student was five dollars an hour, and we didn't have a lot of money in those days, so I started out by taking fifteen minutes. Then as I got to talking to different pilots there who had airplanes, why, I guess they sort of took pity on me trying to fly, you know, being a mother with so many youngsters, and they would let me fly with them in their airplanes. I just started to build up my flying time. I hung around the airport and sort of became a Girl Friday. I gassed and washed planes, helped tie down planes, and [ran] errands, for flying time.

I had a husband who didn't want me to fly and he would come out to the field and be real angry with me and he'd say, "You'd better

Doris Lockness sitting on the wing of her Piper Warrior in the hangar at Orland Haigh Field. Orland, California, 1995.

Doris Lockness is eighty-six years old with thirty-two great-grandchildren but she is still actively flying airplanes and helicopters. She holds advanced ratings in aircraft, helicopters, balloons, rotorcraft, gyroplanes, and gliders, and she is a member or holds office in eleven aviation organizations including the United Flying Octogenarians, OX5 Aviation Pioneers, and the Women Airforce Service Pilots. She has received national and international recognition for her outstanding contributions to aviation: one of her most recent awards was the Elder Statesmen of Aviation award from the National Aeronautical Association.

Doris Lockness flying her Piper Warrior. Orland, California, 1995.

get out of that plane. You're going to leave our children motherless." So he didn't think too kindly of my flying, because really, in those days—this was 1939—there weren't too many women flying. It's not like nowadays; I think that his idea was that something might happen to me and then he'd be left with the children or something like that. But, my gosh, my baby is sixty-two now, and they're not motherless yet, and I've been flying all these years.

The woman's role was different, it was home and family, and cooking, dishes, and household chores. I was the only woman in that area flying, and on Sundays the cars would come out and line up and [people would] just sit in their cars, the curiosity seekers, and watch *that woman* out at the airport flying. That crazy woman who wants to fly airplanes.

We didn't have a whole lot of money in those days, in 1939. We had a refrigerator, a Kelvinator, that had a meter on top of it and you drop quarters in there to keep it running. It was always a toss-up, whether I was going to drop my quarters in there to keep that refrigerator running or use that money to go fly.

Howard Hughes used to fly his airplane and would land at our airport in Wilmington, California. His plane was a Sikorsky S-38 Amphibian, and when it was rough out on the ocean, he couldn't land. He would come in and land at our airport because it was close by. We would take care of his plane, tie it down and refuel it. He was always very pleasant and never talked very much. He was very quiet. He always wore his hair

long, not compared to what they do these days, but for those days. He always wore tennis shoes. He usually had a nice-looking girl with him, usually a redhead. It was real nice to tie his plane down and be of service [to him]. I always thought that he might—thank us, you know, tip us or something like that, for time on his aircraft, but he never did. I found out later that he didn't carry any money with him.

I was up flying the day Pearl Harbor was bombed. I had just taken off from the field, and a military plane from Reeves Field was flying and sort of circled my J-3 Cub and motioned that I go down, so I thought, "What have I done? I must have done something terrible." When I landed, they told me Pearl Harbor had just been bombed and that all flying was off anyplace on the West Coast and for 150 miles inland.

We all were so patriotic in those days and we wanted to do everything we could when the war broke out. I wanted to do my bit. I heard about the WASPs and that Jacqueline Cochran was recruiting female pilots. I thought this was a great opportunity to fly. I just had to go. So I sent for an application and I filled it out, of course, and sent it in. I was surprised I was accepted, because I had four children and I put down my family on the application. So it didn't go over too well at home. My mother-in-law, she was very progressive and she always liked me, and she said, "Well, go ahead, Doris. I'll take care of the family while you're gone." So I said, "Well, that's great." So I went off to war. It was something that I wanted to do, but it was very difficult for me. [My first husband] didn't approve at all. He filed for divorce. It's not like nowadays; there's a lot of women in the aviation careers and they have families. But in those days, it wasn't quite the thing to do.

If you're going to learn anything about a new airplane or a different airplane, you don't learn it as rapid as a younger person. I think maybe you slow up a little bit. I've always been rather active and fast on the controls. I don't have too much trouble that way. I try to fly two or three times a week, according to the weather. You know, with all aviation there's a lot of bookwork, a lot of study. Every time you get a rating, you're deep in the books, and then you're taking your written tests and you're taking your flight tests. I think that flying over the period of years keeps you alert, keeps your mind going.

I think everybody, if their health gets bad, they know it's time to stop flying, just for their own good. But if my health was still good and it was just something maybe that they figured I was too old to fly or something like that, well, then I'd take up the hot air balloon or glider or Ultralight, because I could fly those without a medical.

When I started out flying, it was a feeling of freedom from my home duties and chores. Four young children can keep you kind of busy, so when I flew, I felt a little bit of freedom from everything that was going on. In aviation, you just want to be in the air as much as you can. The more you fly, the more you want to fly, and if you don't fly for a while, you miss it. It's just something that gets into your system. I guess it's a flying bug. I really didn't have that good support

background when I was twenty-nine that a lot of pilots have, but I just made up my mind that was something that I wanted to do. There wasn't anything that could stop me, not even an angry husband and four youngsters.

I can see a lot of changes over the period of years. One of them is the Federal Aviation regulations and all the rules they've made. [In 1939 or 1940] we'd fly out in the desert . . . and there was a little ranch out there [that] we called "Mom and Pop's." It was an old couple [who] lived out there, and they used to fix breakfast for the pilots on Sunday morning. I was flying out there with another pilot in an American Eagle; that's an old biplane. We ran off this runway and hit some cactus and tore fabric off the lower wing. So we got a bedsheet from Mom and made some flour and water paste, and put this big piece of bedsheet on there. By the time we were through with breakfast, why, our flour and water paste was all dried. We used to do a lot of things like that. You don't do that nowadays.

Well, I've had an interesting, exciting life, and I think the most I've done is aviation, flying. I've used just about all my time for that every year. I go to a lot of FAA safety seminars, because I learn something new at every one. You know, the world moves so fast, it kind of goes by us, and if you don't keep current, you're lost. I think that pertains to other things as well as aviation. I know I just got a word processor. Gave up my nice electric typewriter, but I thought this was a step forward.

EILEEN COLLINS

Astronaut *Born November 19, 1956*

I don't really think from day to day [about being] a woman pilot. I'm a shuttle pilot, and I don't get treated any different. The primary job of the pilot is to back up the commander. I am his right-hand man, so to speak. In addition to backing him up in the flying duties, I am also responsible primarily for the main engines, the auxiliary power units, the hydraulic system, the electrical system, and the fuel cells. He's responsible for the computers, which keep the spacecraft flying, and he's also responsible for the environmental system—the air, the cooling, the water—I need to understand the types of malfunctions that could happen, and if those malfunctions do happen, how to recognize them and fix them. I need to know his systems as well as he does.

Our crew is doing our first simulator [practice session] together in the suit next week, which is why I had the suit fit today. The first time you are in the suit in the simulator, it's very difficult, and that's why we train. By the time we fly we want to be comfortable with seeing switches, reaching switches, running procedures, and just your overall sense of where you are in the orbiter with the suit on.

Pretend you're typing on a typewriter. Now, put on a big heavy pair of gloves that you would wear in a winter snowstorm, and then try to type. You're going to have problems. It's very similar flying. When you've got your hand on the stick, you can feel what you're doing. It's normally very sensitive. When you put on a big glove, you can't feel it as well, and it's more difficult to fly. We train with the gloves on so we can get familiar with what it's really going to be like on the day we fly the shuttle.

No one in my family flew. I got interested in flying because my dad would take us up to the airport on the weekends and we would sit in the car and watch airplanes take off. It doesn't sound like a

....

Eileen Collins adjusting her helmet during a pressure suit fitting. NASA, Johnson Space Center, Houston, Texas, 1994.

Lieutenant Colonel Eileen Collins, U.S. Air Force, became the first woman in history to pilot the space shuttle. Her rookie flight aboard *Discovery* STS-63 in February 1995 also marked the beginning of the United States' involvement with Russia's space station *Mir*. Growing up in Elmira, New York, the "Soaring Capital of the World," Collins was inspired to pursue a career in aviation. She entered the U.S. Air Force for her flight training and was selected for the astronaut program while attending Air Force test pilot school at Edwards Air Force Base, California, from which she graduated in 1990. She resides in Houston with her husband and daughter.

Eileen Collins during a pressure suit fitting prior to her space flight. NASA, Johnson Space Center, Houston, Texas, 1994.

very exciting weekend to most people, but to me it was great. We'd go up to Harris Hill [in Elmira, New York] and have a picnic up there, and we'd go to the glider field and watch gliders take off. I never could figure out how they could stay up there without engines, but eventually I started studying about flying and learning about weather. I'd go to the library and check out books on flying just because I was interested and I was curious as to what the pilots were doing up there. From there, I started reading books about military flying. I read about World War II and the Korean War and Vietnam, and I became very interested in military flying, although at the time military pilots were only men.

I did not come from a privileged background. Our family struggled financially as I was growing up. My parents supported me in my flying lessons, but they said, "We want you to learn how to fly, Eileen, but we can't afford it. If you want to do it, go for it, but you've got to earn the money on your own." And I did. With my jobs, I didn't buy clothes, I didn't go out and party all that much with my friends. I didn't have any glamour jobs. I worked at a snack bar at a hospital, then I worked at a catalog showroom, I sold jewelry and clock radios and sports equipment. In college I had a job at a pizza place, where I made subs and pizza and I waited tables. I saved my money. And then when I was nineteen, I took it up to the airport. It took me three years to save the money I needed, but they taught me how to fly. And with that forty hours of flying, I applied to the Air Force, and they accepted

me into pilot training in 1978.

That year, 1978, was also notable in that it was when NASA picked their first women astronauts. They picked six mission specialists. When I saw that in the news, it was planted in my mind: I can be an astronaut someday. They're now taking women. It became a very realistic goal of mine. I had the degree in math that I needed. I needed to join the Air Force, and get my flying time. If I wanted to be a pilot, I needed to get a master's degree. I needed to go to test pilot school and become a test pilot. That was all something I was going to enjoy anyway, so it sort of worked out.

I never really talked very much about the fact that I wanted to be an astronaut. I just applied to the program, and I figured, if they want me, they'll accept me.

I was in test pilot school when I interviewed to be an astronaut and also when I got the phone call telling me that I had been accepted into the program. I always thought that if it happened, if I was accepted, I would just scream and yell and jump up and down and be totally elated and have a party. You know, it wasn't like that. It was a huge relief when they called me and said, "You've been accepted." I had finally achieved my goal.

Eventually down the road I'd like to fly as a commander. I am eligible to be a commander, since I was hired here at NASA as a pilot. That is really a position that you need to earn based on your performance. We'll have to see how the space program's going a few years down the road.

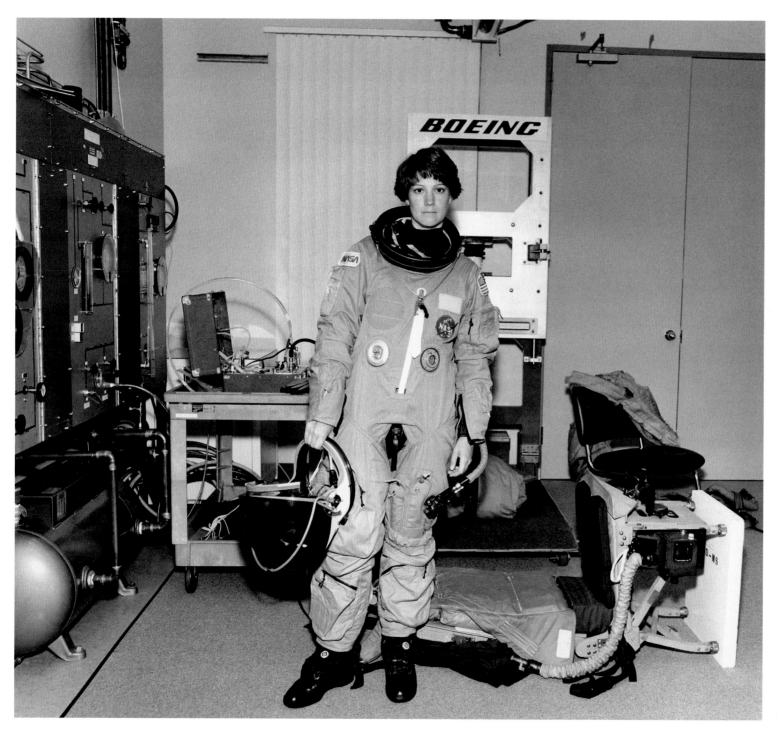

PATRICIA JENKINS

Helicopter Pilot *Born October 2, 1943*

Our cattle hear this helicopter overhead so often that they just kind of glance around and "Oh, it's just her again." They don't run out of just sheer fright. Other people's cattle do. That's how I know when I have other people's cattle, and it makes it a lot easier to get them separated, because the others just take off in a dead run like a spilled bag of marbles.

The only time my cowboys really appreciate me is when I take the hilltops. We are running through mountain range up there, and in the summer we have to move our cattle up the hills, we're working with steep, rocky hillsides. I have to push all the cows who have grazed way up to the top of these rocky, shale hillsides. I don't run them off or tumble them off, I just get up there and hover in front of them, and they get the idea and they turn around and start going back down the hill.

I've watched the cowboys and learned how to move cattle the way they do on horseback. I don't just barge into a bunch of cows. I work from perimeters and push one cow at a time toward the center of a group of cattle, staying as far away from them as I can and still getting them to move. I don't want them to run. Cows walk at about a five-mile-an-hour pace, and that's fine with me. I just stay in a slow, dusty, old hot hover behind them, and let them walk at their own speed.

Five years into the marriage, my husband decided he wanted to learn to fly, and I said, "Well, if you're going to learn, I'd better learn, too." So we traded beef for flying lessons. I was raising children and doing "housewifely" things and hated it. I was bored to death. So the airplane was a good brainteaser for me. The flying was just what I needed. I could finally do something. I hadn't finished school and I don't have a degree. So flying was the next

Patricia Jenkins on her cattle ranch property with her Hughes 300 helicopter named Woodstock *in the background. Diamond, Oregon, 1995.*

Pat Jenkins works as a flying "cowboy" in her Hughes 300 helicopter hovering over fifteen hundred head of beef cattle on her ranch in Diamond, Oregon. The terrain she flies over is 100,000 acres of high desert consisting of sage brush, deep canyons, steep rocky hillsides, and rattlesnakes. From the helicopter she monitors fence lines, water holes, moves cattle and checks their health, and carries up to one hundred pounds of salt lick. Her responsibilities on the ground include being the ranch cook and book-keeper. Jenkins travels two hundred miles to meet with other women pilots at the Boise, Idaho, chapter Ninety-Nine meetings. Jenkins is a vegetarian.

best thing that I could do and feel okay about myself living out here.

A neighbor here, a rancher who had a very small ranch, bought a Hughes 300 and had it nearby, and Dick [husband] had occasion to ask him to fly him up to the mountain quickly and back. He fell in love with the dumb thing and came home and raved about how efficient and how quick [it was] and blah, blah, blah. So the more he talked it up, the more I dragged my feet, and didn't think we could really justify the expense of owning and operating a helicopter. So we decided we'd really research it and put a pencil to it, and it still looked very iffy, but we started shopping around for helicopters. We bought a ship before we ever even took a lesson.

I thought it was awful. First of all you can take off with no air speed, you can turn with no pedal, you can climb with no airspeed. It's about as stable as a champagne cork. All the aerodynamics fit the same as a fixed-wing, but the actual controlling of the helicopter I found to be really tough. About ten hours into the flight instruction, I wanted to throw my hands in the air and say, "Forget it, I'm never going to learn this."

We had already purchased the machine. I already had a job with it. I had to learn how to fly it. It's all mine. Yes, that's my cow pony. I'm supposed to do it all myself. Yep. My palomino, as I call her. It was either that or we had to hire a bunch of buckaroos to do what I was now already designed to do.

If you hire more cowboys, then you have to have housing, ground vehicles, and horses for them. Then the payroll, and it's just a

Patricia Jenkins hovering in her Hughes 300 helicopter on her cattle ranch in Diamond, Oregon, 1995.

horrendous amount of money. So that's how we were justifying the helicopter, by eliminating those other expenses. Well, it turned out that by the end of the summer, we realized the helicopter could do a lot more than we thought, more than we'd ever penciled in when we were trying to figure out how valuable it might be.

The minute I leave, I don't get altitude, I have to stay close to the ground all the time, because my job is observation. I have to be sure fences are up, the wires are on all the fences, the gates are closed or open as they're supposed to be. Almost all my work is done very close to the ground. I'd say ten, twenty feet. I have to do visual observation of my cattle, making sure what they look like, if they're thin or comfortable, if they look lost or if they're in the wrong fields. You have to get close enough to read an earmark, which is a little clip, or a brand on the hip if you think they're not your cattle.

I've had to learn that you can't make a cow move where she doesn't want to go if she's without her calf. She'll turn around and run right back to find her baby. If you go slowly enough that they can walk in pairs, then you can take them anywhere. I just get big streams of cows going down to the lower part of the little valleys and canyons, and then the cowboys ride along the bottom of the canyon and move the cattle up to the next pasture. They love that, but otherwise they're not terribly thrilled with the helicopter. It takes away a lot of the riding time, and the cowboys love that, to go out and live in a cabin, cook for themselves, no women in camp, and stay there for days and days.

So with the helicopter, I can go out and check the cattle in the morning, get back here in time to cook lunch, because I'm the crew cook for the hay crew, and they don't like just chicken salad sandwiches. They want meat and potatoes and gravy dinners at lunchtime. So it's a real effort to do the cooking. Then I'm back in the machine in the afternoon, and can do the fencing or move cattle or whatever is needed to be done.

On our private posted land, we don't like people deer hunting in there because our cattle are there during deer season. So I patrol it, so to speak, and I don't really enjoy that because hunters are not very happy when you're flying overhead, and I'm terribly exposed in that little machine and they're carrying guns. They haven't shot at me as far as I know, but I wouldn't say they never would. We're out West.

We have beautiful wildlife. When I go to work, I'll fly over antelope and deer right in my own field, and little coyotes are out there and they always scatter and run from the helicopter. Beautiful birdlife all over the place. There are a few places where I have to shut down and leave the machine and walk on trails to get to places that I have to open and/or close gates that are in the juniper woods. So then I get to walk in the silence out there. It's wonderful, listening to the elk calling back and forth. I have a great commute.

Patricia Jenkins outside her
helicopter hangar in
Diamond, Oregon, 1995.

MARSHA NEAL

Aeronaut *Born September 7, 1957*

We're always talking to people on the ground. We can hear them a little clearer because sound travels up. People don't anticipate that, and you'll yell down and say something and they'll say, "What? Where did that come from?" I remember one time, we were flying relatively low over a neighborhood looking for a place to come in and land. And there was a woman, trying to film us flying overhead, running around the backyard looking out through this movie camera and she was running into everything. She'd run into the picnic table, into the clothesline, into the bushes. And we'd tell her, "Oh, look out, you're going to run into the tree!"

It's fun to land, and, of course, from an advertising perspective we always are trying to fly around the city, landing in neighborhoods. Since it's relatively calm, when we fly, we can come down, say, in a cul-de-sac or in the middle of a street if the power lines are buried. You can land in people's driveways and their backyards. It's just really fun to come in and see the astonished look on people's faces.

Then there are times when you've got other thoughts running through your mind if it's not quite that easy. I did a flight at the U.S. nationals last year, and they brought out two passengers from a retirement home. I had these two women who were in their eighties and it was really very breezy. So I'm zipping along the treetops looking for a nice place to land, where I can come in and do it softly. I could just see these two little old ladies crumpled up in the bottom of the basket, because if you've got a breeze pushing you, you come in, and you have to set it down a little hard, and you drag along, and so forth. And the whole time, they didn't understand it. I ended up doing this wonderful landing behind a tree break in a little grass field.

Marsha Neal piloting her hot air balloon. Statesville, North Carolina, 1994.

Since 1984, Marsha Neal has been president and owner of La Conquista Hot Air Balloons, an aero advertising business. She manages the national Cadillac balloon team as well as numerous regional contracts. She also teaches, sells, and races both hot air and gas balloons. The aeronaut has won many national and international competitions in hot air balloons. She has also competed in the World Gas Balloon Race in 1986, 1988, and 1994 and in the prestigious Gordon Bennett gas ballooning race in Europe in 1987. She is the vice president of the Balloon Federation of America.

Marsha Neal after landing her hot air balloon. Statesville, North Carolina, 1994.

Cows are really funny, because they'll come up and just want to sniff and poke around and see what's going on. Generally they may get a little skittish at first and kind of run around, but then it always turns into curiosity. By the time you've got the balloon laying over, you're trying to shoo them away so they're not walking on it.

The biggest chance for doing any damage on a balloon is when you're inflating it. If it's real windy, and you get a gust and it blows the fabric into the flame, you can burn a hole in it — thus, you scrub the flight. Or on landing, if you take it down in a tight area and you have a tree that's got a sharp limb, you can put a tear in it. But during flight, nothing is going to happen.

I think I'm almost a purist when it comes to gas ballooning because to me — there's nothing to compare it to. There's no burner noise, nothing. The wonderful thing about gas ballooning is that you can fly all day and all night. The most incredible thing flying over the countryside is that you can hear this network of dogs talking to each other. I mean, you can pick up the communication, just sitting up there listening, and you can hear very distinctly any car driving down the road.

Fred Hyde and I had competed and won the National Championship in this country two years in a row. We just really seem to make a good team flying together and were winning all the events. That afforded us the opportunity to compete in the World Championships and then also in the Gordon Bennett long-distance race, which we did. The first trip over in '87 we did the flight out of Austria and landed down in Yugoslavia.

We had permission to go into Yugoslavia, but the organizers couldn't obtain any air charts beyond just the northern rim, which was on the sectional that we were using. So we took a road map and sort of transposed some longitude and latitude lines on it as best we could figure and just flew with that. Anyway, we flew all day at about 15,000 feet and just felt good about the distance that we were doing, but by the end of the day we knew we couldn't go another night. So we set up for landing and were really just into central Yugoslavia, and came down. Did a real nice landing in a little farm field. And instantly there were all these farmers out there. And we've got this balloon full of gas that we had to get vented out. So our first thing is to get them away from the balloon with their cigarettes so that it doesn't blow up, which we managed to do. They sort of understood, but there was no language exchange whatsoever.

Then I was doing something in the basket, I heard all this shouting. I turned around and saw that this little car had driven up and it had "Militia" written on the side. So nobody knows we're out here. These guys show up with machine guns. Fred is like an absentminded professor kind of personality. Not much rattles him. He was looking for his hat and he pulled out my camera and, of course, they grabbed this camera out of his hand. And now they know we're on a spy mission or something. They took us to this little jailhouse in this little village. The balloon is lying there, it's full of avionics, all this equipment we've borrowed and rented from pilots.

The telephone lines were dead. But, we got through the next day. We were able to get them in touch with people who could tell them what was going on. The farmers had slept with that balloon all night. And they had just sort of camped out, watched everything. Everything was there. It was fine. They helped us pack it up. Again, we've got no real language exchange. You don't get that when you go backpacking. That's just one of the most wonderful things about ballooning—it puts you in situations with people that you just would not get to any other way.

The World Championship was the following year, in 1988. I just happened to be seven months pregnant. I was big. The Europeans are not as open-minded about that kind of thing, and most of the pilots involved in gas ballooning in Europe are men. They really couldn't believe that I could do such a thing. I mean, they were astonished. A lot of pilots that I had come to know would say, "Gee, are you really sure you need to be doing this?" I would just assure them that if there was a chance of uncertain weather that we would take precautions.

I think it's going to be real interesting what Margaret [daughter] decides to do with the influence of ballooning in her life. We took a little girlfriend along [for a flight] and they sat down in the basket and they were telling stories and it was like, how you used to pretend everything was like a little house when you were young. They'd look out every once in a while, trying to grab the tops of the trees as we came over. I think it's going to be interesting to see if it's something that she'll pick up.

....
Marsha Neal's silhouette outside an inflated hot air balloon. Statesville, North Carolina, 1994.

190

Acknowledgments

First and foremost, my true gratitude belongs to the pilots and astronauts in *Women and Flight*.

I especially want to thank Michael Burton at Ilford Photo for his support of in-kind donations of film and paper and to the Smithsonian Institution Women's Committee for their grant toward interview transcription. Special thanks to Pratt & Whitney and United Technologies Corporation, who generously supported the traveling exhibit.

To my coworkers Mark Avino and Terry McCrea, at the NASM Photography Department, I owe many thanks. I am grateful to Dorothy Cochrane, who was vital for her guidance, editorial advice, and her introduction to the book. I thank Bob Craddock for his encouragement and assistance, and Trish Graboske for her publishing support. From the NASM Archives and Library, to Brian Nicklas, who always made his expertise in aircraft and network of pilots available, and to Phil Edwards, who suggested a project on women pilots, I am grateful. There were many individuals at the National Air and Space Museum who assisted me at various stages in the project: Alice Adams, Barbara Brennan, Gwendolyn Crider, Bob Curran, Tom Crouch, Linda Ezell, Jeff Goldstein, Jacqueline Grazette, Martin Harwit, Dave Heck, Jo Hinkel, Kristine Kaske, Linda King, Don Lopez, Beatrice Matkovic, Valerie Neal, Scotty O'Connell, Bob Padgett, David Romanowski, Anne Seeger, Tom Soapes, and Ron Wagaman. A special word of appreciation to LeRoy London and Wendy Stephens for their encouragement and support.

I am especially thankful to Deborah G. Douglas of NASA Langley Research Center, who not only shared her advice and expertise on the topic of women and aviation, but so generously contributed funding at the early stages of the project. I am indebted to the various organizations that have located pilots for me, especially the members of the Organization of Black Airline Pilots, the members of the Ninety-Nines Inc. International Women Pilots, and Jean Ross Howard-Phelan, who was especially helpful, as were the members of the Whirly Girls Inc. International Women Helicopter Pilots.

I wish to thank the many individuals who helped at the Public Affairs Offices of the United Sates Navy, the United States Army, and the United States Air Force. A special note of thanks to Pat Malpass and Andrew Patnesky at NASA Public Affairs at Johnson Space Center, Leann Swieczkowski at Army Public Affairs at the Pentagon, and to Connie Summers at Army Public Affairs in Heidelberg, Germany. In Russia, I am indebted to the assistance of Elena Zheltova, Ruslan Kuzmin, Lena Zabalueva in Moscow, and to Andre Majboroda and Mike Baker at the Cosmonaut Training Center in Star City. I want to acknowledge Anne Kluttz for her assistance in Norfolk, Virginia, and Statesville, North Carolina, and to thank the entire crew at the Flying Circus in Bealeton, Virginia.

I owe special appreciation to Hugh Talman and Jim Wallace for their assistance at the Smithsonian Institution Office of Printing and Photographic Service; Janice McNeil, Charlotte Cohen, and the staff at the Smithsonian Institution Traveling Exhibition Service; and staff members at the Smithsonian Institution Office of Exhibits Central.

It was a privilege to work with Chuck Hyman and Anne Masters on the book design and with editors Patricia Fidler and Dorothy Williams at Bulfinch Press, Little, Brown and Company. I wish to acknowledge Deborah Reid at Techni-Type Transcripts, for her excellent transcription of the interviews, and Barbara Borden for encouraging me to write the text.

To my family, and dear friends, especially to John Russo, Lissa Stewart, Anna Fili-Astofone-Potts, and Mangai Balasegaram, thank you for your support. Finally, I would like to make special reference to Brian Lanker's book *I Dream a World*, to which I looked for inspiration throughout the duration of the project.